60 Digital Moneymakers

Launch Your Digital Product & Building a Lucrative Empire

By
M.I.Fazil

Table of contents

28. Language Learning Apps with AI-Powered Chatbots
29. Augmented Reality (AR) Filters
30. High-Fidelity Mockups & Prototypes
31. Machine Learning Algorithms
32. Cybersecurity Tools
33. Custom Content Management Systems (CMS)
34. Advanced Online Courses with Personalized Learning Paths
35. Big Data Analytics Platforms
36. Interactive simulations for complex systems
37. Adaptive Learning Platforms that tailor content to individual student needs
38. Stock Market Prediction Models
39. 3D-printable object designs
40. High-quality, realistic 360° video tours
41. Custom Architectural Renderings
42. Original Sound Design Libraries
43. Internet of Things (IoT) Applications
44. Artificial Intelligence (AI) Chatbots
45. Custom Enterprise Software
46. Industry-Specific Data Analysis Tools
47. Immersive Learning Experiences
48. Personalized Learning Management Systems (LMS) with Advanced Reporting
49. Custom E-commerce Stores with Advanced Personalization Features
50. Digital Twins of Physical Products or Systems
51. Ebooks on Common Interests
52. Printable Planners & Templates
53. Stock Photos for Specific Niches
54. Social Media Templates

Introduction

The digital landscape is brimming with opportunity. Imagine creating a product that sells itself, requires minimal upkeep, and generates income while you sleep. That's the magic of digital products! This book is your roadmap to unearthing your own personal "digital goldmine."

Within these pages, we'll delve into 60 unique and effective strategies for turning your skills and passions into profitable digital products. Whether you're a seasoned entrepreneur or just starting your journey, there's something here for everyone. We'll explore a vast array of options, from educational courses and creative assets to printables and software solutions.

This book isn't just about ideas; it's about empowering you to take action. We'll provide practical guidance on everything from product creation and pricing to marketing and building a loyal customer base. You'll learn how to leverage the power of online platforms, build a strong brand identity, and scale your digital empire.

Are you ready to unlock your earning potential and become a master of the digital marketplace? Let's dive in and discover the wealth of possibilities that await!

1. Customizable Design Templates

Customizable design templates are pre-made design elements that can be easily modified to create unique and professional-looking designs. They offer a valuable shortcut for both creative professionals and businesses, saving time and resources while maintaining a polished aesthetic.

Benefits of Customizable Design Templates:

Increased Efficiency: Templates eliminate the need to start a design from scratch, allowing creators to focus on customization and content.

Cost-Effective Solution: Using templates is often more affordable than hiring a designer for every project.

Consistency & Branding: Templates help maintain a consistent visual identity across various designs, reinforcing brand recognition.

Accessibility for Non-Designers: Even those with limited design experience can create professional-looking graphics using user-friendly templates.

Types of Customizable Design Templates:

Graphic Design Templates: These include social media posts, logos, flyers, posters, email templates, and presentations.

Web Design Templates: Pre-built website layouts that can be customized with colors, fonts, and images to suit specific needs.

Print Design Templates: Templates for brochures, business cards, postcards, and other printed materials.

Video Editing Templates: Pre-made video intros, outros, transitions, and lower thirds that can be easily customized with your brand elements and video content.

Key Features of Customizable Design Templates:

Editable Text & Fonts: You can change the text content and choose from various fonts to match your brand or project theme.

Customizable Colors: Modify the color palettes of the templates to align with your brand identity or project requirements.

Replaceable Images & Graphics: Easily swap out placeholder images and graphics with your own visuals.

Resizable Layouts: Some templates allow resizing to fit different output formats like social media posts or presentations.

Popular Platforms for Customizable Design Templates:

Canva: A user-friendly platform with a vast library of free and paid templates for various design needs.

Adobe Spark: Offers free, easy-to-use templates for creating social media graphics, short videos, and web stories.

Freepik: A marketplace with a wide selection of free and premium design resources, including customizable templates.

Shutterstock: Provides royalty-free stock photos, videos, and music, along with a growing collection of customizable design templates.

Unbounce: Offers landing page templates specifically designed for conversion optimization.

Tips for Using Customizable Design Templates Effectively:

Choose high-quality templates: Opt for well-designed templates with clean layouts and professional typography.

Maintain brand consistency: Customize templates using your brand colors, fonts, and logos to ensure a cohesive brand image.

Focus on high-quality visuals: Use relevant and professional-looking images and graphics to enhance your designs.

Don't be afraid to experiment: While templates offer a base, feel free to customize them creatively to achieve a unique look.

By leveraging the power of customizable design templates, creatives and businesses can streamline their design workflow, save valuable time and resources, and create impactful and visually appealing designs.

2. High-Quality Stock Photos

High-quality stock photos are a valuable digital product with the potential to generate consistent income. They cater to a vast market of individuals and businesses who need professional-looking images for various online and offline purposes. Whether you're a seasoned photographer or just starting out, creating and selling stock photos can be a rewarding way to monetize your skills and creativity.

The Allure of Stock Photos:

Universal Demand: Stock photos are in constant demand by websites, blogs, social media platforms, marketing materials, advertisements, and more.

Passive Income Potential: Once uploaded to stock photo platforms, your photos can generate income every time someone downloads them.

Scalability: You can build a library of images over time, increasing your earning potential with each new photo added.

Low Barrier to Entry: While high-quality equipment helps, even basic cameras can capture images suitable for stock photo platforms.

Qualities of Successful Stock Photos:

Technical Excellence: Sharp focus, proper exposure, and good composition are essential for professional appeal.

Concept & Relevance: Images should be visually appealing and relevant to popular search terms and current trends.

Diversity & Inclusivity: Feature a broad range of subjects, people, and settings to cater to a wider audience.

Emotional Connection: Images that evoke positive emotions or tell a story tend to be more popular.

Keywords & Titles: Use relevant keywords and descriptive titles to ensure your photos are easily discoverable through platform searches.

Monetizing Your Stock Photos:

Microstock Platforms: These platforms like Shutterstock, Adobe Stock, and iStock offer a royalty-based model, where you earn a commission every time someone downloads your image.

Macrostock Agencies: These agencies like Getty Images and Alamy require higher quality standards and exclusivity. They offer higher per-image payouts but may have stricter submission guidelines.

Direct Licensing: Sell licenses directly to businesses for specific uses. This requires building relationships with potential clients.

Building a Successful Stock Photo Business:

Identify Your Niche: Focus on specific themes or subjects where there's a high demand but low competition.

Invest in Learning: Brush up on photography basics, composition techniques, and keyword research.

Curate a Diverse Portfolio: Build a collection of images covering various topics and styles to attract a wider audience.

Maintain Consistency: Regularly upload new content to stay relevant and increase discover ability.

Track Performance: Analyze which photos perform well and adjust your strategy based on data.

Conclusion:

High-quality stock photos are a valuable digital product with the potential to generate a steady stream of income. By understanding the market demands, focusing on quality and relevance, and choosing the right platform, you can establish a successful stock photo business in the thriving digital world.

3. Advanced Photoshop Actions & Presets

For professional photographers and graphic designers, advanced Photoshop actions and presets can be a game-changer. These tools automate complex editing tasks, saving countless hours and offering a consistent, high-quality aesthetic. But did you know these advanced tools can also be a lucrative source of income? Let's delve into the world of creating and selling advanced Photoshop actions and presets for digital profit.

Unleashing the Power of Advanced Actions & Presets:

Enhanced Workflow: Automate repetitive editing tasks like color correction, sharpening, adding effects, and resizing. This frees up time for focusing on creative aspects of image editing.

Consistent Style: Presets ensure a consistent visual style across multiple images, ideal for photographers with a signature look or designers working on branding projects.

Non-Destructive Editing: Actions and presets work on non-destructive layers, allowing easy adjustments and maintaining the original image quality.

The Allure of Advanced Tools for Income Generation:

Targeted Market: Advanced tools appeal to busy photographers and designers who value efficiency and consistent results.

Premium Value Proposition: Advanced functionalities like complex one-click edits, batch processing, and creative effects command a premium price compared to basic presets.

Recurring Revenue: Build a library of presets and offer them as individual downloads or bundled packages for recurring income.

What Makes Advanced Actions & Presets Stand Out?

Functionality: Go beyond basic edits. Offer features like selective color adjustments, advanced noise reduction, HDR toning, or artistic effects.

Customization Options: Allow users to customize the presets to their liking through sliders, drop downs, or masking capabilities.

Compatibility: Ensure compatibility with popular Photoshop versions and consider offering versions for other editing software.

Documentation & Support: Provide clear instructions for installation and use. Consider offering video tutorials or support channels for troubleshooting.

Monetizing Your Expertise:

Standalone Downloads: Sell individual actions or presets directly from your website or through marketplaces like Envato Elements.

Subscription Model: Offer a subscription service with access to a growing library of advanced tools and exclusive content.

Bundled Collections: Create thematic packages of presets catering to specific photography genres (e.g., weddings, portraits, landscapes) or design styles.

Building a Successful Business with Advanced Tools:

Sharpen Your Skills: Master advanced Photoshop techniques and understand the needs of your target audience.

High-Quality Previews: Showcase the impact of your actions and presets using captivating before-and-after visuals.

Targeted Marketing: Promote your tools to relevant communities like photographer forums, design blogs, and social media groups.

Customer Reviews & Testimonials: Encourage satisfied customers to leave positive reviews to build trust with potential buyers.

Stay Updated: Keep your tools compatible with the latest Photoshop versions and consider offering updates with new functionalities.

With the right approach, advanced Photoshop actions and presets can become a valuable asset in your digital product portfolio. By combining your editing expertise, a focus on user needs, and effective marketing, you can transform your skills into a thriving income stream in the ever-evolving world of digital design.

4. 3D Models & Animations

3D models and animations are the building blocks of a vast and visually stunning digital realm. From captivating video games and immersive virtual experiences to product design and architectural visualizations, these digital creations are in high demand. This note explores the world of 3D models & animations, highlighting their potential as valuable digital products for income generation.

The Power of 3D:

Realistic Representation: 3D models accurately represent real-world objects or create entirely new ones, allowing for detailed visualization and interaction.

Animation Brings It to Life: Animations breathe life into 3D models, adding movement, storytelling elements, and emotional depth to digital experiences.

Versatility Across Industries: 3D models and animations are used in various fields like architecture, engineering, product design, film, animation, video games, and virtual reality.

Monetizing Your 3D Expertise:

Marketplace Sales: Sell your 3D models and animations on online marketplaces like TurboSquid,

CGTrader, and Adobe Stock. These platforms offer royalty-based earnings or fixed pricing models.

Direct Client Commissions: Work directly with clients on specific projects, creating custom 3D models and animations for their needs. This offers higher earning potential but requires marketing and client acquisition efforts.

Subscription Services: Offer a subscription service providing access to a library of your 3D models and animations, ideal for generating recurring income.

Creating Marketable 3D Models & Animations:

High Quality & Optimization: Ensure your models are visually appealing, well-optimized for different software, and have a clean topology for smooth use.

Focus on Specific Niches: Identify niches with high demand but low competition, like architectural models for specific building types or character models for a particular genre.

Variety & Customization: Offer variations of your models with different textures, materials, or poses to cater to diverse user needs. Consider offering customizable options for added value.

Keywords & Metadata: Optimize your models with relevant keywords and detailed descriptions to ensure easy discoverability on marketplaces.

Building a Successful 3D Business:

Master the Software: Proficiency in 3D modeling software like Blender, Maya, or ZBrush is essential for creating high-quality assets.

Invest in Learning Resources: Continuously hone your skills by taking online courses, attending workshops, and staying updated with industry trends.

Build a Portfolio: Showcase your best creations in an online portfolio to attract potential clients and demonstrate your capabilities.

Community Engagement: Actively participate in online forums, social media groups, and 3D communities to build connections and market your work.

By leveraging your 3D modeling and animation skills, you can create a lucrative income stream. By focusing on quality, marketability, and continuous learning, you can position yourself as a valuable asset in the ever-growing demand for creating captivating digital experiences.

5. Vector Illustrations

Vector illustrations, those clean and infinitely scalable graphics, are a powerful tool for designers and a hot commodity in the digital age. But did you know your vector skills can be a lucrative source of income? This article dives into the various ways you can turn your vector mastery into a steady stream of cash.

Monetization Avenues for Vector Artists:

• Stock Illustration Marketplaces: Become a contributor to platforms like Shutterstock, Adobe Stock, or Freepik. These sites allow you to upload your creations and earn royalties every time someone downloads your vector.

• Freelance Illustration: Showcase your portfolio on freelance platforms like Upwork or Fiverr and connect with businesses or individuals needing vector illustrations for websites, marketing materials, presentations, or product packaging.

Print-on-Demand Services: Partner with print-on-demand platforms like Redbubble or Society6 to sell your vector designs on t-shirts, mugs, phone cases, and other merchandise.

• Direct Client Sales: Build a strong online presence and target specific industries that heavily rely on vector graphics. Pitch your services directly to marketing agencies, design studios, or e-commerce businesses.

• Create and Sell Vector Asset Packs: Compile themed vector packs (e.g., social media icons, UI elements, infographics) and sell them through your own website or platforms like Creative Market.

• Subscription-Based Services: Offer a subscription service where clients pay a monthly fee for access to a library of your vector illustrations.

Tips for Success:

• Sharpen Your Skills: Invest in honing your vector software proficiency (Adobe Illustrator is a popular choice) and explore advanced techniques.

• Develop a Signature Style: Create a unique and recognizable visual style that sets you apart from other vector artists.

• Keyword Research: Understand what kind of vector illustrations are in high demand. Use relevant keywords when uploading your work to stock platforms or building your portfolio.

• Market Yourself Effectively: Build a strong online presence with a professional website or social media profiles showcasing your best work.

• Network and Build Relationships: Connect with other designers, participate in online communities, and attend industry events to increase your visibility.

• Price Competitively: Research the going rates for vector illustration services in your region and adjust your pricing accordingly.

• Provide Excellent Customer Service: Be responsive to client inquiries, offer revisions when needed, and build trust for long-term collaborations.

Remember, building a sustainable income stream with vector illustrations takes dedication and effort. However, with the right skills, strategy, and hustle, you can turn your passion for vector art into a profitable career.

6. Original Music Scores & Sound Effects

The power of sound is undeniable. Original music scores and sound effects have the ability to elevate any visual experience, creating emotional impact, enhancing storytelling, and leaving a lasting impression. This note explores the potential of original music scores and sound effects as valuable digital products for income generation in the digital age.

The Power of Sound:

Emotional Connection: Music and sound effects evoke emotions, immersing viewers or listeners in the narrative and creating a stronger connection with the content.

Enhanced Storytelling: The right music and sound effects can subtly guide the audience's emotional journey, adding depth and nuance to the story.

Versatility Across Media: Original scores and sound effects are in high demand for various media formats, including films, video games, animations, documentaries, podcasts, and even mobile apps.

Monetizing Your Musical Expertise:

Marketplace Sales: Sell your original music scores and sound effects on online marketplaces like AudioJungle, Pond5, and Envato Elements. These platforms offer royalty-based earnings or fixed pricing models.

Direct Client Commissions: Compose custom music scores and sound libraries for specific projects, working directly with filmmakers, game developers, or video creators. This offers higher earning potential but requires active client prospecting.

Subscription Services: Offer a subscription service providing access to a library of your sound effects and royalty-free music scores, ideal for generating recurring income.

Creating Marketable Music & Sound Effects:

High-Quality Audio: Ensure your music scores and sound effects are professionally produced, with clean recordings, and well-mixed audio mastering.

Genre & Mood Variety: Create music and sound effects catering to various genres and moods, like suspenseful thrillers, heartwarming comedies, or epic fantasy adventures.

Usability & Customization: Offer sound effects in different formats with clear descriptions and metadata for easy integration into various editing software. Consider providing customizable elements within scores for user flexibility.

Keyword Optimization: Use relevant keywords and descriptive titles to ensure your music and sound effects are easily discoverable through platform searches.

Building a Successful Sound Business:

Music Composition Skills: Develop strong music composition skills and a broad understanding of music theory, orchestration, and different musical styles.

Sound Design Expertise: Learn sound design principles like recording, editing, manipulating audio, and creating realistic sound effects.

Production Value: Invest in high-quality audio equipment and recording software to ensure professional sound quality.

Portfolio & Demo Reel: Create a strong portfolio showcasing your musical compositions and sound effects libraries to attract potential clients.

Industry Networking: Network with video creators, filmmakers, and game developers to build valuable connections and explore potential collaborations.

By leveraging your musical talent and sound design skills, you can create a sustainable income stream with original music scores and sound effects. Focusing on quality, genre variety, and discoverability can help you establish yourself as a go-to resource for soundtracks that set the tone for any digital experience.

7. Custom Fonts

Custom fonts are more than just stylish text; they are the building blocks of visual identity. They can elevate a brand's message, set the tone for a website, or add a touch of personality to a creative project. This note explores the world of custom fonts, highlighting their potential as valuable digital products for income generation.

The Allure of Custom Fonts:

Brand Differentiation: A unique font can help a brand stand out from the crowd, creating a memorable visual identity and strengthening brand recognition.

Enhanced User Experience: Custom fonts can improve readability and user experience, especially on websites or in design projects with specific visual styles.

Versatility Across Media: Custom fonts can be used for logos, websites, printed materials, marketing campaigns, and even digital products themselves.

Monetizing Your Font Design Skills:

Marketplace Sales: Sell your custom fonts on online marketplaces like Creative Market, MyFonts, and FontSpring. These platforms offer royalty-based earnings or fixed pricing models.

Direct Font Licensing: License your fonts directly to businesses for exclusive use in their branding or marketing materials. This offers higher earning potential but requires active client acquisition efforts.

Subscription Services: Offer a subscription service providing access to a library of your custom fonts, ideal for designers and creatives seeking a variety of styles.

Creating Marketable Custom Fonts:

Technical Expertise: Master font design software like FontLab Studio or Glyphs to create technically sound and visually appealing fonts.

Understand Design Trends: Stay updated on current design trends and user preferences to create fonts that cater to the evolving needs of the market.

Readability & Functionality: Balance creativity with functionality. Ensure your fonts are clear, legible, and work well across different sizes and platforms.

Character Sets & Licensing: Offer fonts with various character sets to cater to different languages and consider offering different licensing options for individual or commercial use.

Building a Successful Font Business:

Develop Your Design Style: Develop a unique design style that sets your fonts apart. Experiment with different aesthetics like modern, classic, playful, or elegant.

Strong Portfolio Showcase: Create a captivating portfolio website to showcase your fonts in various design applications.

Marketing & Community Engagement: Actively market your fonts on social media platforms, design blogs, and online communities frequented by graphic designers.

Customer Service & Support: Offer excellent customer service by providing clear licensing information, technical support, and updates for your fonts.

By leveraging your font design skills and understanding the market needs, you can establish a lucrative income stream. By focusing on creativity, functionality, and effective marketing, you can transform your passion for lettering into a thriving digital product business.

8. E-books with Interactive Elements

In today's digital age, readers crave engaging and interactive experiences. E-books with interactive elements go beyond static text and images, offering a dynamic and immersive reading journey. This note explores the exciting world of interactive e-books and their potential as valuable digital products for income generation.

The Power of Interactive E-books:

Enhanced Engagement: Interactive elements like quizzes, polls, clickable images, and embedded audio/video clips keep readers engaged and actively participating in the content.

Improved Knowledge Retention: Interactive elements promote deeper understanding by allowing readers to test their knowledge and explore topics further.

Accessibility & Personalization: Interactive features can cater to different learning styles and provide personalized learning paths within the e-book.

Monetizing Interactive E-books:

Direct Sales: Sell your interactive e-books directly through your own website or e-commerce platforms like Shopify or Gumroad. This offers full control over pricing and profit margins.

Subscription Services: Offer access to a library of your interactive e-books through a subscription model, generating recurring income.

Educational Marketplaces: Sell your e-books on platforms like Udemy or Skillshare, reaching a wider audience of learners and educators.

Creating Marketable Interactive E-books:

Content Expertise: Master the subject matter of your e-book and identify knowledge gaps that interactive elements can address.

Engaging Narrative: Craft a compelling narrative that seamlessly integrates interactive elements, maintaining a smooth reading flow.

Technical Skills: Learn e-book creation tools like iBooks Author, InDesign, or specialized interactive e-book development platforms.

Usability & Accessibility: Ensure your interactive features are user-friendly, function across different devices, and are accessible for readers with disabilities.

Building a Successful Interactive E-book Business:

Market Research: Identify target audiences who would benefit from interactive learning and the specific topics that are in demand.

Prototype & Testing: Develop a prototype of your e-book with interactive elements and gather user feedback to ensure a seamless and engaging experience.

Effective Marketing: Promote your e-books through social media marketing, targeted advertising, and collaborations with relevant bloggers or influencers.

Subscription Model Value: Offer additional features or exclusive content within your subscription model to incentivize recurring customers.

By combining your subject matter expertise with design and technical skills, you can create interactive e-books that stand out in the crowded e-book market. By focusing on reader engagement, value proposition, and effective marketing, you can transform your knowledge into a profitable digital product.

9. Productivity Apps

Productivity apps are digital tools designed to streamline tasks, manage time effectively, and enhance overall workflow. With the ever-growing demand for organization and efficiency in our fast-paced world, productivity apps present a lucrative opportunity for income generation. Here's a detailed breakdown of creating and selling productivity apps for profit:

The Allure of Productivity Apps:

Universal Appeal: People across various professions and personal lives seek ways to be more productive, making the market vast and diverse.

Recurring Revenue Potential: Many productivity apps offer subscription models, allowing for consistent income streams.

Scalability: As your app user base grows, your earning potential increases without requiring significant additional investment.

Types of Popular Productivity Apps:

Task Management Apps: Help users organize tasks, set deadlines, track progress, and collaborate efficiently.

Time Management Apps: Offer tools for time tracking, scheduling, focus optimization, and identifying productivity bottlenecks.

Habit Formation Apps: Support users in building positive habits, overcoming procrastination, and achieving goals.

Note-Taking and Brainstorming Apps: Provide features for capturing ideas, organizing notes, and collaborating on projects.

Project Management Apps: Designed for teams to manage projects, assign tasks, track progress, and share files.

Monetizing Your Productivity App:

Freemium Model: Offer a basic free version with limited features alongside a premium version with advanced functionalities for a subscription fee.

In-App Purchases: Provide additional features or customization options within the app that users can purchase with a one-time fee.

Subscription Model: Offer a tiered subscription with different levels of access and features, catering to diverse user needs and budgets.

Developing a Successful Productivity App:

Identify a Specific Need: Focus on a particular pain point or inefficiency that your app can address effectively.

User-Centric Design: Prioritize a clean, intuitive user interface and a user-friendly experience for optimal adoption.

Integrations & Compatibility: Consider offering integrations with popular calendars, cloud storage services, or other productivity tools.

Data Security & Privacy: Implement robust security measures and ensure user data privacy compliance with relevant regulations.

Marketing Your Productivity App:

App Store Optimization (ASO): Optimize your app store listing with relevant keywords and compelling visuals to boost discover ability.

Social Media Marketing: Promote your app on relevant social media platforms and engage with potential users.

Content Marketing: Create blog posts, articles, or video tutorials that showcase the benefits of your app and target specific productivity challenges.

Freemium Strategy: Use the free version of your app as a marketing tool to entice users to upgrade to the premium features.

By addressing a specific need in the productivity landscape and prioritizing user experience, you can create a valuable productivity app. Implementing a thoughtful monetization strategy and effective marketing tactics can help you turn your app into a thriving digital product business.

Additional Tips:

Consider offering a freemium trial to allow users to experience the benefits of the premium features before committing.

Gather user feedback through surveys and reviews to continuously improve your app and stay relevant to user needs.

Explore offering enterprise versions with additional features and security protocols for businesses and organizations.

The world of productivity apps offers a promising path for income generation in the digital age. By focusing on a strong value proposition, well-designed user experience, and effective marketing, you can transform your app idea into a profitable digital asset.

10. E-commerce Plugins & Extensions

E-commerce plugins and extensions are powerful tools that extend the functionalities of existing e-commerce platforms like WooCommerce or Shopify. They cater to a wide range of needs, from enhancing product presentation and payment gateways to improving marketing automation and customer service. This note explores the exciting world of e-commerce plugins and extensions, highlighting their potential as valuable digital products for income generation.

The Allure of E-commerce Plugins & Extensions:

Solve Specific Problems: E-commerce plugins address specific pain points for online store owners, improving functionality and streamlining various aspects of their business.

Increased Demand: With the ever-growing e-commerce landscape, the demand for innovative and effective plugins continues to rise.

Recurring Revenue Potential: Many e-commerce plugins offer subscription-based models, generating consistent income for developers.

Types of Popular E-commerce Plugins & Extensions:

Product Page Optimization: Enhance product pages with features like 360° product views, zoom functionality, and product comparison tools.

Payment Gateways: Integrate additional payment gateways to cater to a wider customer base and offer more payment options.

Shipping & Fulfillment: Simplify shipping processes by integrating with shipping carriers or fulfillment services.

Marketing & Analytics: Provide tools for email marketing automation, abandoned cart recovery, and insightful customer behavior analytics.

Customer Service & Support: Implement live chat functionalities, chatbot integration, and ticketing systems for improved customer interactions.

Monetizing Your E-commerce Plugin Development Skills:

Freemium Model: Offer a basic free version with limited features alongside a premium version with advanced functionalities for a subscription fee.

One-Time Purchases: Sell your plugin for a one-time fee, offering lifetime access or updates for a limited period.

Marketplace Sales: Sell your plugin on established marketplaces like CodeCanyon or the Shopify App Store, reaching a wider audience of store owners.

Developing Marketable E-commerce Plugins:

Identify a Gap in the Market: Focus on a specific need that existing plugins don't adequately address or offer a unique solution with better functionality.

Seamless Integration: Ensure your plugin integrates seamlessly with popular e-commerce platforms and doesn't conflict with other plugins.

User-Friendly Interface: Prioritize a clean and intuitive user interface for both store owners and their customers interacting with the plugin's features.

Technical Support & Updates: Offer reliable technical support and provide regular updates to address bugs, ensure compatibility with platform updates, and introduce new features.

Marketing Your E-commerce Plugin:

Targeted Marketing: Promote your plugin through blog posts, tutorials, and online communities relevant to e-commerce store owners.

Freemium Strategy: Use the free version of your plugin as a marketing tool to attract users and showcase the value proposition of the premium features.

Partner with Influencers: Collaborate with e-commerce influencers or bloggers to promote your plugin to their audience.

Highlight Customer Success Stories: Showcase positive testimonials and success stories from satisfied store owners using your plugin.

By identifying a specific need within the e-commerce ecosystem and developing a well-designed, user-friendly plugin, you can establish yourself as a valuable asset to online store owners. By implementing a thoughtful monetization strategy and effective marketing tactics, you can transform your e-commerce plugin development skills into a thriving digital product business.

Additional Tips:

Offer excellent customer support: Respond promptly to user inquiries and provide helpful documentation to ensure a positive user experience.

Stay updated on e-commerce trends: Continuously adapt your plugins to address evolving customer needs and keep pace with changing e-commerce platforms.

Consider offering white-labeled versions: Provide the option for agencies or other developers to rebrand your plugin for their clients.

The world of e-commerce plugins and extensions offers a lucrative opportunity for developers with a passion for streamlining online store functionalities. By focusing on solving real problems, providing excellent user experience, and effectively marketing your solutions, you can turn your development skills into a sustainable source of income in the ever-growing e-commerce landscape.

11. Custom WordPress Themes

Custom WordPress themes are the digital facades that transform websites. They go beyond pre-built templates, offering a unique design and functionality tailored to a specific brand or purpose. This note explores the exciting world of custom WordPress theme development and its potential as a valuable source of income in the digital age.

The Power of Custom Themes:

Brand Identity & Differentiation: A custom theme reflects a brand's personality and sets it apart from competitors, fostering stronger brand recognition.

Enhanced User Experience: Custom themes can optimize website layouts, navigation, and user interaction, leading to a more engaging and user-friendly experience.

Conversion Optimization: Custom themes can be designed with specific conversion goals in mind, improving lead generation or sales for businesses.

Monetizing Your Theme Development Skills:

Project-Based Pricing: Charge clients a fixed fee for designing and developing a custom theme based on their specific needs and project scope.

Theme Sales: Sell pre-built custom themes directly from your own website or through marketplaces like ThemeForest or TemplateMonster.

Freemium Model: Offer a free basic theme with limited features alongside a premium version with advanced functionalities and ongoing support for a recurring fee.

Crafting Marketable Custom Themes:

Design Expertise: Master design principles like typography, color theory, layout composition, and user interface (UI) design to create visually appealing and user-friendly themes.

WordPress Development Skills: Proficiency in coding languages like HTML, CSS, and PHP is essential for building functional and responsive themes.

Understanding SEO: Integrate best practices for search engine optimization (SEO) within your themes to ensure client websites rank well in search results.

Mobile-First Approach: Develop themes that are fully responsive and optimize for flawless display and user experience across all devices.

Building a Successful Theme Business:

Market Research & Niche Identification: Identify specific niches within the WordPress market where custom themes are in high demand but with less competition.

Portfolio Showcase: Create a high-quality portfolio website showcasing your design skills and the range of custom themes you offer.

Excellent Client Communication: Maintain clear communication with your clients throughout the design and development process to ensure their vision is met.

Ongoing Support & Maintenance: Offer ongoing support and maintenance plans to address client needs after the initial project is complete.

Marketing Your Custom Themes:

Targeted Content Marketing: Create blog posts, tutorials, or video content that showcases your design expertise and provides valuable insights for website owners.

Social Media Marketing: Promote your custom themes and design services on relevant social media platforms like Twitter, LinkedIn, or design communities.

Freemium Strategy: Use the free version of a theme as a marketing tool to attract potential clients and showcase the premium features available.

Offer Free Consultations: Provide free initial consultations to potential clients, allowing them to discuss their website needs and understand how a custom theme can benefit them.

By combining your design expertise with strong development skills and a focus on client needs, you can establish yourself as a valuable asset in the WordPress ecosystem. Implementing a strategic pricing model and effective marketing tactics can help you transform your custom theme development skills into a thriving digital product business.

Additional Tips:

Stay Updated on WordPress Trends: Continuously learn about the latest WordPress features and best practices to ensure your themes are compatible with platform updates.

Security & Performance Optimization: Prioritize theme security and ensure your themes are lightweight and load quickly to deliver optimal website performance.

Offer Customization Options: Allow some level of customization within your pre-built themes to cater to individual client preferences.

The world of custom WordPress themes offers a dynamic and rewarding path for designers and developers. By focusing on creating visually stunning, user-friendly themes that cater to specific market needs, and by effectively marketing your services, you can turn your passion for WordPress into a profitable digital product business.

12. Mobile Apps

Mobile apps have become an indispensable part of our daily lives. They offer entertainment, streamline tasks, connect us with information and services, and present a lucrative opportunity for income generation in the digital world. This note explores the exciting world of mobile app development and its potential as a valuable source of income from digital products.

The Allure of Mobile Apps:

Massive User Base: With billions of smartphones in use worldwide, the potential audience for your app is vast and diverse.

Recurring Revenue Potential: Freemium models with in-app purchases or subscription services can generate consistent income streams.

Scalability: Once developed, your app can reach a global audience with minimal additional investment compared to physical products.

Types of Profitable Mobile Apps:

Gaming Apps: Casual or strategy games with engaging mechanics and in-app purchases for virtual items, power-ups, or ad removal.

Productivity Apps: Tools that enhance organization, scheduling, task management, or streamline daily routines, often with freemium or subscription models.

Entertainment Apps: Music streaming, video streaming, social media platforms, or educational apps with freemium models or premium subscriptions.

E-commerce Apps: Apps that allow users to browse products, make purchases, and manage orders directly from their smartphones.

Utility Apps: Apps that solve specific problems like photo editing, language translation, travel booking, or fitness tracking, often with freemium models.

Monetizing Your Mobile App Development Skills:

Freemium Model: Offer a basic free version with limited features and monetize through in-app purchases for additional features, premium content, or ad removal.

Subscription Model: Provide a full range of features through a recurring subscription fee, offering different tiers with varying functionalities.

Paid App Downloads: Sell your app for a one-time upfront fee, though this model faces stiff competition from free apps.

In-App Advertising: Integrate targeted advertising within your app, earning revenue based on user clicks or impressions.

Developing Marketable Mobile Apps:

Identify a Market Need: Focus on a specific problem, task, or interest that your app can address effectively and offer a unique solution compared to existing apps.

User-Centric Design: Prioritize a clean, intuitive user interface (UI) and user experience (UX) for optimal usability and user engagement.

Platform Optimization: Develop native apps for iOS and/or Android, ensuring they are optimized for each platform's specific features and user preferences.

Offline Functionality: Consider offering core functionalities even when users are offline to enhance user experience in situations with limited internet connectivity.

Marketing Your Mobile App:

App Store Optimization (ASO): Optimize your app store listing with relevant keywords, compelling visuals, and clear descriptions to improve discover ability.

Social Media Marketing: Promote your app on relevant social media platforms and engage with potential users through targeted campaigns.

Content Marketing: Create blog posts, articles, or video tutorials that showcase your app's benefits and target specific user needs.

Influencer Marketing: Collaborate with relevant mobile app reviewers or influencers to promote your app to their audience.

By understanding the market demands, developing a user-friendly and valuable app, and implementing effective marketing strategies, you can transform your mobile app development skills into a thriving digital product business.

Additional Tips:

Gather user feedback: Actively solicit user feedback through surveys and app reviews to continuously improve your app and stay relevant to user needs.

Offer excellent customer support: Respond promptly to user inquiries and provide helpful resources within the app to ensure a positive user experience.

Consider offering a free trial: Provide a limited-time free trial of premium features to entice users to subscribe or purchase the full version.

Stay updated on mobile trends: Continuously learn about new technologies, user behavior patterns, and platform updates to keep your app competitive.

The world of mobile app development offers immense potential for income generation. By focusing on a strong value proposition, exceptional user experience, and effective marketing strategies, you can turn your app idea into a profitable digital product that empowers users while enriching your income stream.

13. Web Scraping Tools

Web scraping tools automate the process of extracting data from websites. While ethical considerations are crucial, these tools can be harnessed to create valuable digital products for businesses and individuals. This note explores the potential of web scraping tools as a source of income in the digital age.

The Power of Web Scraping Tools:

Data Collection & Aggregation: Scrape data from various websites, consolidating it into a structured format for analysis and insights.

Market Research & Competitor Analysis: Gather product pricing, customer reviews, or competitor marketing strategies to inform better business decisions.

Lead Generation & Prospecting: Extract contact information or relevant user data to build qualified lead lists for targeted marketing campaigns.

Data-Driven Content Creation: Scrape relevant data for market research reports, product comparisons, or industry trend analysis.

Monetizing Your Web Scraping Expertise:

Develop & Sell Web Scraping Tools: Create user-friendly web scraping tools with various features and functionalities for different user skillsets, offering them for purchase with one-time fees or subscriptions.

Provide Web Scraping Services: Offer custom web scraping services for businesses, scraping specific data sets based on their needs and delivering the data in a clean, usable format.

Curated Data Feeds & Market Research Reports: Scrape, analyze, and curate data into insightful reports or data feeds that businesses can purchase to gain a competitive edge.

Building Marketable Web Scraping Tools:

Ease of Use: Prioritize a user-friendly interface that allows users with varying technical skills to leverage the scraping capabilities.

Flexibility & Customization: Offer features for users to define specific scraping targets, data formats, and filtering options based on their needs.

Data Cleaning & Export: Ensure the scraped data is cleaned for accuracy and offer export options in various formats like CSV, JSON, or Excel for easy integration with other tools.

Ethical Considerations: Adhere to ethical web scraping practices, respecting website robots.txt guidelines and avoiding overloading servers with excessive scraping requests.

Building a Successful Web Scraping Business:

Market Research & Niche Identification: Identify specific industries or use cases where businesses require web scraping solutions and cater your tools or services to those needs.

Technical Expertise: Develop a strong understanding of web scraping techniques, handling different website structures, and overcoming anti-scraping measures ethically.

Data Security & Compliance: Ensure robust data security practices and build trust with users by being transparent about data handling and complying with relevant data privacy regulations.

Stay Updated on Technology: Continuously learn about new web technologies and adapt your tools to handle evolving website structures and scraping challenges.

Marketing Your Web Scraping Products & Services:

Content Marketing: Create blog posts, tutorials, or video content that educate potential users about web scraping and how your tools can benefit them.

Industry-Specific Marketing: Target your marketing efforts towards businesses in industries where web scraping offers significant advantages.

Freemium Model: Offer a limited free version of your scraping tool with basic features to entice users and showcase the value proposition of the paid version.

Case Studies & Testimonials: Showcase successful client projects or highlight case studies demonstrating the positive impact your web scraping solutions have had on businesses.

By developing user-friendly web scraping tools, offering valuable data-driven services, and prioritizing ethical practices, you can establish yourself as a trusted resource in the web scraping landscape. By implementing strategic marketing tactics and staying ahead of the technological curve, you can transform your expertise into a profitable digital product business.

Important Note: Remember, it's crucial to act ethically when web scraping. Always respect robots.txt guidelines, avoid overloading servers, and prioritize data accuracy and user privacy.

14. Cloud-Based Design Software

Cloud-based design software has revolutionized the design industry. Offering accessibility, collaboration, and powerful tools from any device, these platforms present a lucrative opportunity for income generation in the digital age. This note explores the exciting world of cloud-based design software and its potential as a valuable source of income from digital products.

The Allure of Cloud-Based Design Software:

Accessibility & Scalability: Users can access their work and collaborate with team members from anywhere with an internet connection, fostering remote work and project flexibility.

Subscription-Based Revenue: Cloud-based software allows for recurring income through subscription models, offering different tiers with varying features and storage capacities.

Reduced Software Costs: Eliminates the need for users to purchase expensive software licenses, making design tools more accessible to a wider audience.

Types of Popular Cloud-Based Design Software:

Graphic Design: Tools for creating logos, illustrations, social media graphics, presentations, and marketing materials. (e.g., Canva, Adobe Creative Cloud)

User Interface (UI) & User Experience (UX) Design: Platforms for prototyping mobile apps, websites, and designing user interfaces for optimal user experience. (e.g., Figma, Adobe XD)

3D Modeling & Animation: Cloud-based software for creating 3D models, animations, and product visualizations. (e.g., Tinkercad, Sketchfab)

Video Editing & Motion Graphics: Platforms for editing videos, creating motion graphics, and adding visual effects for marketing campaigns or social media content. (e.g., Adobe Premiere Pro, DaVinci Resolve)

Monetizing Your Cloud-Based Design Software Development:

Subscription Model: Offer tiered subscription plans with varying storage capacities, feature sets, and collaboration tools to cater to individual users, freelancers, and design teams.

Freemium Model: Provide a limited free version with basic features to attract users and showcase the value proposition of the premium features available in paid subscriptions.

In-App Purchases: Offer additional features or design assets within the software for purchase, allowing users to customize their experience based on specific project needs.

Integrations & Partnerships: Integrate your software with other design tools or cloud storage services to expand functionality and offer bundled solutions.

Developing Marketable Cloud-Based Design Software:

Seamless User Interface: Prioritize a clean, intuitive user interface (UI) that allows users with varying design experience levels to create effectively within the software.

Collaboration Features: Integrate real-time collaboration tools like chat, co-editing, and version control to facilitate teamwork on design projects.

Cloud Storage & Security: Provide secure cloud storage for design assets, ensuring data integrity and accessibility across devices.

Device Optimization: Ensure smooth functionality across various devices, including desktops, laptops, and tablets.

Marketing Your Cloud-Based Design Software:

Content Marketing: Create blog posts, tutorials, or video content that showcase the capabilities of your software and target specific design challenges users face.

Freemium Strategy: Use the free version of your software to attract new users and convert them to paying subscribers by highlighting the benefits of premium features.

Social Media Marketing: Promote your software on relevant social media platforms and engage with the design community through targeted campaigns.

Freelancer & Design Agency Partnerships: Partner with freelance designers and design agencies to promote your software and offer them benefits like discounted subscriptions.

By focusing on user needs, delivering a user-friendly and collaborative design experience, and implementing effective marketing strategies, you can transform your cloud-based design software development skills into a thriving digital product business.

Additional Tips:

Offer excellent customer support: Respond promptly to user inquiries and provide helpful documentation and tutorials within the software.

Stay updated on design trends: Continuously update your software with new features, design tools, and integrations to stay relevant in the ever-evolving design landscape.

Offer free trials: Provide limited-time free trials of premium features to entice users to experience the full potential of your software and convert them to paying subscribers.

Community Building: Foster a community around your software through forums, webinars, or online events, allowing users to connect, share knowledge, and provide valuable feedback for product development.

The world of cloud-based design software offers a promising path for income generation. By focusing on a strong value proposition, exceptional user experience, and effective marketing, you can transform your design software into a cloud-based business that empowers designers and fuels your income stream.

15. API Integrations

The world of digital products relies heavily on seamless communication between different applications and services. This magic is often powered by APIs (Application Programming Interfaces). By enabling data exchange and functionality sharing, API integrations unlock a vast potential for income generation in the digital product landscape. This note explores the exciting world of API integrations and how they can be leveraged to create valuable digital products.

The Power of API Integrations:

Enhanced Functionality: APIs allow your digital product to connect with other services, extending its functionalities and offering a more comprehensive user experience.

Data-Driven Value: Integrations enable data exchange, allowing your product to leverage external data sources for features like market analysis, personalized recommendations, or real-time updates.

Streamlined Workflows: APIs can automate tasks and data exchange between different platforms, saving users time and effort within your digital product.

Monetizing Your API Integration Expertise:

Develop & Sell Pre-Built Integrations: Create pre-built integrations that connect your own digital product or service with popular platforms (e.g., payment gateways, social media platforms) and sell them to other businesses for a one-time fee or subscription.

API Management & Consulting: Offer consulting services to help businesses design and implement API integration strategies for their digital products, ensuring optimal data flow and functionality.

Custom Integration Development: Develop custom API integrations for specific client needs, connecting their digital products with desired external services for a project-based fee.

Building Marketable API Integrations:

Seamless Connectivity: Ensure your pre-built integrations connect flawlessly with the target platforms, offering a smooth and reliable user experience.

Clear Documentation & Support: Provide comprehensive documentation and technical support to empower users to utilize your integrations effectively within their products.

Security & Data Privacy: Prioritize robust security measures and adhere to data privacy regulations when handling data exchange through your integrations.

Scalability & Performance: Design integrations that can handle large data volumes and maintain optimal performance under high user loads.

Building a Successful API Integration Business:

Market Research & Niche Identification: Identify specific niches or industries where API integrations can significantly improve existing digital products and target your services or pre-built solutions accordingly.

Technical Expertise: Develop a strong understanding of different API protocols, security considerations, and best practices for building robust and scalable integrations.

Partnerships & Community Engagement: Build partnerships with other digital product developers and actively contribute to the API developer community to enhance visibility and foster trust.

Stay Updated on Technology: Continuously learn about evolving API standards, emerging platforms, and security best practices to keep your integrations future-proof.

Marketing Your API Integration Expertise:

Content Marketing: Create blog posts, articles, or video tutorials that educate potential clients about the benefits of API integrations and showcase your expertise.

Case Studies & Client Testimonials: Highlight successful client projects where your API integrations have significantly enhanced their digital products.

Industry Events & Conferences: Participate in industry events and conferences to network with potential clients and showcase your API integration solutions.

Open-Source Contributions: Contribute to open-source projects related to API development, demonstrating your technical skills and building credibility within the developer community.

By understanding the power of API integrations, developing well-designed solutions, and implementing effective marketing strategies, you can transform your API integration expertise into a lucrative digital product business. Remember, success lies in focusing on seamless connectivity, providing valuable resources, and staying at the forefront of evolving API technologies.

16. Blockchain-Based Applications

Blockchain technology, with its decentralized ledger system and tamper-proof data storage, is revolutionizing various industries. This note explores the exciting world of blockchain-based applications (dApps) and their potential as a source of income from digital products.

The Allure of Blockchain-Based Applications:

Decentralization & Trust: Eliminates the need for central authorities, fostering trust and transparency within applications.

Enhanced Security: Blockchain's immutable ledger ensures data security and minimizes the risk of fraud or manipulation.

Programmable Functionality: Smart contracts automate processes and enforce predefined rules within dApps.

Types of dApps with Income Potential:

Decentralized Finance (DeFi): Create user-owned financial platforms enabling peer-to-peer lending, borrowing, and asset trading, often with opportunities to earn interest or fees.

Non-Fungible Tokens (NFTs): Develop marketplaces or platforms for minting, trading, and managing NFTs, potentially earning commission fees on transactions.

Supply Chain Management: Design dApps for tracking goods through the supply chain, providing transparency and tamper-proof records, and potentially charging businesses subscription fees.

Data Storage & Sharing: Develop dApps for secure and decentralized data storage, offering users control over their data and potentially charging for data storage or access.

Monetizing Your Blockchain Development Skills:

Develop & Sell dApps: Create and sell pre-built dApps for specific functionalities (e.g., DeFi platforms, NFT marketplaces) to businesses or individuals for a one-time fee or licensing model.

Smart Contract Development: Offer custom smart contract development services, tailoring contracts to meet specific business needs and charging project-based fees.

Consulting & Advisory Services: Provide consulting services to help businesses understand and integrate blockchain technology into their operations, earning fees for your expertise.

Developing Marketable Blockchain Applications:

Real-World Use Cases: Focus on developing dApps that address specific problems and offer a clear value proposition compared to existing solutions.

User-Friendly Interface: While blockchain technology can be complex, prioritize an intuitive user interface (UI) for easier adoption by users with varying technical backgrounds.

Security & Scalability: Ensure robust security measures are in place to protect user assets and dApp functionality. Design dApps with scalability in mind to handle increasing user loads.

Regulatory Compliance: Stay updated on evolving blockchain regulations and ensure your dApps comply with relevant legal frameworks.

Building a Successful Blockchain Business:

Market Research & Niche Identification: Identify specific industries or use cases where blockchain technology can offer significant advantages and tailor your dApp development or services accordingly.

Community Building: Actively engage with the blockchain developer community, contribute to open-source projects, and build trust within the ecosystem.

Stay Updated on Technology: The blockchain landscape is rapidly evolving. Continuously learn about new protocols, security best practices, and emerging trends to keep your skills and dApps relevant.

Partnerships & Collaborations: Partner with other blockchain developers or businesses to expand your reach and expertise, potentially co-developing dApps or offering complementary services.

Marketing Your Blockchain Expertise:

Content Marketing: Create blog posts, articles, or video tutorials that explain blockchain concepts and showcase your development expertise.

Webinars & Presentations: Participate in industry events, conferences, or online webinars to educate potential clients and showcase your knowledge of blockchain applications.

Open-Source Contributions: Contribute to open-source blockchain projects, demonstrating your technical skills and building credibility within the developer community.

Case Studies & Client Testimonials: Highlight successful projects where your blockchain applications have delivered value to businesses or organizations.

By understanding the potential of blockchain technology, developing secure and user-friendly dApps, and implementing effective marketing strategies, you can transform your blockchain development skills into a thriving digital product business. Remember, success hinges on addressing real-world needs, prioritizing security and compliance, and staying ahead of the curve in this dynamic technological landscape.

17. In-Depth Industry Reports

The digital product industry is experiencing explosive growth, driven by increasing consumer adoption of online platforms and a desire for convenient, on-demand access to information and services. This report delves into the various revenue streams generated by digital products, explores trends shaping the market, and analyzes the potential future of this dynamic sector.

Market Size and Growth

The digital product industry is projected to reach a staggering $74 billion by 2025 [Source: Thinkific]. A J.P. Morgan study highlights this significant growth potential. The overall digital commerce market, which encompasses digital products alongside physical goods, is expected to reach a value of $19.43 trillion by 2032, reflecting a compound annual growth rate (CAGR) of 15.8% [Source: Precedence Research].

Types of Digital Products and Revenue Models

E-learning and Online Courses: This is a booming segment, offering in-depth instruction in a wide range of subjects. Revenue comes from one-time course purchases, subscriptions, and freemium models with premium content upgrades.

Software as a Service (SaaS): Cloud-based software solutions provide ongoing value to users, generating recurring revenue through monthly or annual subscriptions.

Ebooks and Digital Publications: The convenience and affordability of ebooks have driven strong market growth. Revenue streams include one-time purchases, subscriptions for access to libraries of ebooks, and freemium models with a limited selection of free titles.

Music, Movies, and Games: Digital downloads and streaming services have revolutionized entertainment consumption. Revenue comes from individual song or movie purchases, subscriptions for unlimited access, and in-app purchases within games.

Digital Templates and Stock Assets: Designers, photographers, and videographers can sell their creations as downloadable assets, generating income from one-time purchases or subscriptions for ongoing access.

Trends Shaping the Market

Growing Mobile Adoption: Consumers are increasingly using smartphones and tablets to access digital products, driving the need for mobile-friendly platforms and payment options.

Subscription Economy: The popularity of subscription models provides a predictable revenue stream for businesses and ensures ongoing value for customers.

Focus on User Experience: Creating a seamless and enjoyable user experience is crucial for attracting and retaining customers in a competitive marketplace.

Content Personalization: Personalization of content and recommendations based on user preferences enhance engagement and drive sales.

The Rise of the Creator Economy: Platforms are emerging that empower individuals to create and sell their own digital products, fostering a diverse and dynamic marketplace.

Future Potential

The future of the digital product industry is bright. With continued technological advancements, such as artificial intelligence and virtual reality, new and innovative digital products will emerge, catering to evolving consumer needs and preferences. Continued growth in internet penetration and the increasing adoption of mobile devices will further fuel market expansion.

Key Considerations for Businesses

Identify a niche market: Focus on a specific target audience and their unique needs to create a successful digital product.

Develop high-quality content: Provide valuable and engaging content that solves problems or fulfills a specific desire for your target audience.

Embrace effective marketing: Utilize targeted marketing strategies to reach your ideal customers and build brand awareness.

Leverage technology: Explore how technology can enhance your digital product and streamline the user experience.

Stay adaptable: Be prepared to adapt your offerings and business model to keep pace with evolving market trends and user preferences.

Conclusion
The income potential from digital products is undeniable. By understanding the market landscape, identifying trends, and implementing effective strategies, businesses can capitalize on this thriving industry and generate significant revenue streams.

18. Financial Modeling Templates

Financial modeling is essential for any business selling digital products. It allows you to forecast revenue, expenses, and profitability, helping you make informed decisions about pricing, marketing, and product development. Here's a breakdown of key elements when building a financial model for digital products:

Types of Templates:

Basic Income Statement: This is a starting point, tracking income from product sales (one-time or subscriptions), recurring revenue streams (e.g., SaaS subscriptions), and any additional income sources (e.g., affiliate marketing). It also captures your cost of goods sold (COGS), which for digital products might include development costs or platform fees.

Subscription Model Template: This template delves deeper into subscription-based income, projecting customer acquisition costs, churn rate (percentage of customers who cancel), average revenue per user (ARPU), and customer lifetime value (CLTV). It helps you assess the long-term profitability of your subscription model.

Freemium Model Template: This model factors in free users alongside paying customers. Track conversion rates from free to paid plans, analyze engagement metrics of free users, and forecast potential upgrade rates to paid subscriptions.

Marketplace Model Template: If you operate a platform for selling digital products by others, this template incorporates vendor fees, commissions on sales, and marketing costs associated with attracting sellers and buyers to your platform.

Key Assumptions:

Pricing Strategy: Input your pricing structure for different product types or subscription tiers.

Sales Forecast: Project your expected sales volume based on historical data, market trends, and marketing efforts.

Customer Acquisition Cost (CAC): Estimate the cost associated with acquiring new customers through various marketing channels.

Customer Churn Rate: Forecast the percentage of customers who cancel subscriptions or stop using your product in a given period.

Variable Costs: Factor in any costs that fluctuate with sales volume, such as transaction fees or payment processing charges.

Financial Outputs:

Revenue: Total income generated from product sales and subscriptions.

Profit Margin: Percentage of revenue remaining after accounting for COGS and operating expenses.

Break-even Point (BEP): The sales volume required to cover all your costs and generate zero profit.

Customer Lifetime Value (CLTV): The total revenue a customer is expected to generate throughout their relationship with your business.

Internal Rate of Return (IRR): The discount rate that makes the net present value (NPV) of all future cash flows from your product equal to zero. This helps you evaluate the project's profitability.

Additional Considerations:

Marketing Spend: Model the impact of different marketing budgets on customer acquisition and sales growth.

Development Costs: Factor in ongoing development costs for product maintenance, updates, and potential new features.

Scalability: Consider how your financial model can adapt to potential future growth scenarios.

Resources:

Pre-built Templates: Several online resources offer pre-built financial model templates for digital products. Popular options include Financial Planning & Analysis (FP&A) software like Excel: [Excel spreadsheet software] or Google Sheets with add-on templates.

Consulting Services: Financial consulting firms can help you build a customized financial model tailored to your specific business needs.

Conclusion
Financial modeling is a powerful tool for businesses selling digital products. By utilizing the right templates, assumptions, and outputs, you can gain valuable insights into your financial health, forecast future performance, and make strategic decisions that maximize your revenue and profitability.

19. Marketing Automation Tools

In the competitive world of digital products, efficient marketing is crucial for driving sales and generating income. Marketing automation tools can be game-changers, streamlining your efforts and nurturing leads into paying customers. Here's how these tools can empower your digital product business:

Benefits of Marketing Automation:

Increased Efficiency: Automate repetitive tasks like email marketing, social media scheduling, and lead nurturing campaigns, freeing up your time to focus on strategic initiatives.

Personalized Customer Journeys: Craft targeted messaging based on user behavior and preferences, creating a more engaging and relevant experience.

Improved Lead Conversion: Automate lead nurturing sequences that keep potential customers engaged and move them closer to a purchase decision.

Data-Driven Marketing: Track campaign performance and analyze user data to gain insights and optimize your marketing efforts for better results.

Scalability: Automation allows you to manage a growing audience efficiently without needing to significantly increase manual effort.

Key Features for Digital Product Businesses:

Email Marketing Automation: Create automated email sequences to welcome new subscribers, deliver valuable content, promote your products, and nurture leads.

Landing Page Creation: Design high-converting landing pages to capture leads and promote specific products or offers.

Website Tracking and Analytics: Track user behavior on your website to understand customer interests and optimize the user experience.

Segmentation and Targeting: Create targeted marketing campaigns based on user demographics, purchase history, and website behavior.

Workflow Automation: Set up automated workflows that trigger specific actions based on user behavior, such as sending follow-up emails after someone abandons a shopping cart.

Webinar and Event Management: Automate registration, reminders, and follow-up communication for webinars or online events promoting your products.

CRM Integration: Integrate your marketing automation tool with your CRM (Customer Relationship Management) system to gain a holistic view of your customer interactions.

Popular Marketing Automation Tools for Digital Products:

ActiveCampaign: Caters well to e-commerce businesses with features like abandoned cart automation and win-back campaigns.

ConvertKit: Tailored for creators and educators selling digital products, offering landing page creation and email marketing automation.

Drip: Focuses on e-commerce marketing automation, with features like product recommendations and personalized abandoned cart emails.

Podia: An all-in-one platform specifically designed for selling online courses, memberships, and digital downloads, with built-in marketing automation features.

Teachable: Another online course platform with marketing automation tools for promoting your courses and nurturing leads.

Choosing the Right Tool:

Business Needs: Consider your specific marketing goals, budget, and the size of your customer base.

Product Type: Choose a tool that integrates well with your existing platforms and caters to the marketing needs of your digital product.

Ease of Use: Evaluate the user interface and learning curve to ensure the tool fits your team's technical expertise.

Scalability: Consider how the tool will accommodate your future growth plans.

Conclusion:
Marketing automation tools are powerful assets for businesses selling digital products. By automating tasks, personalizing customer journeys, and leveraging data-driven insights, you can streamline your marketing efforts, improve conversion rates, and ultimately increase your income from digital products.

20. SEO Optimization Tools

Search Engine Optimization (SEO) is critical for driving organic traffic to your website or landing pages, which can significantly impact your income from digital products. SEO optimization tools can help you identify relevant keywords, optimize your content, and track your website's search engine ranking, ultimately increasing your online visibility and attracting potential customers.

Benefits of SEO Tools for Digital Products:

Keyword Research: Discover high-volume, low-competition keywords that your target audience is searching for when looking for products like yours.

Content Optimization: Analyze your content to ensure it incorporates relevant keywords naturally, improving search engine ranking and user experience.

On-Page Optimization: Identify technical SEO issues on your website that might be hindering search engine crawl and indexing.

Competitor Analysis: See what keywords your competitors rank for and develop strategies to outrank them in search results.

Backlink Monitoring: Track backlinks to your website, which are crucial for SEO and establish your website's authority.

Rank Tracking: Monitor your website's ranking for chosen keywords over time to measure the effectiveness of your SEO efforts.

Popular SEO Tools for Digital Products:

Free Tools:

Google Search Console: A free tool from Google that provides valuable insights into your website's search performance, including keyword ranking, technical issues, and backlinks.

Google Keyword Planner: Part of the Google Ads platform, this free tool helps you discover new keyword ideas and analyze search volume and competition levels.

Paid Tools:

SEMrush: An all-in-one SEO toolkit offering comprehensive features for keyword research, competitor analysis, backlink monitoring, and on-page optimization.

Ahrefs: Another powerful SEO toolset with advanced features for competitor research, backlink analysis, content optimization suggestions, and rank tracking.

Moz Pro: Provides keyword research tools, link building recommendations, on-page SEO audits, and MozBar, a browser extension for quick SEO insights.

Choosing the Right Tool:

Budget: Free tools offer valuable features, but paid tools often provide more in-depth data and functionalities.

Technical Expertise: Consider your team's SEO knowledge and the tool's user interface complexity.

Specific Needs: Evaluate which features are most important for your digital product and marketing goals (e.g., keyword research, competitor analysis, rank tracking).

Optimizing Your Digital Products for SEO:

Targeted Content: Create high-quality content that addresses your target audience's pain points and incorporates relevant keywords naturally. This could include blog posts, tutorials, product descriptions, or case studies that showcase the value of your digital product.

Technical SEO: Ensure your website is mobile-friendly, has a fast loading speed, and uses clean website architecture with proper URL structure and title tags.

Link Building: Earn backlinks from high-authority websites in your niche to improve your website's credibility and search ranking.

Conclusion:
By leveraging SEO optimization tools and implementing effective SEO strategies, you can increase your digital product's visibility in search engine results pages (SERPs). This translates to more organic traffic, improved brand awareness, and ultimately, greater potential income from your digital offerings. Remember, SEO is an ongoing process, so regularly revisit your keyword strategy, monitor your performance, and adapt your tactics to stay ahead of the curve.

21. HR Management Software

While HR (Human Resources) software might not seem directly connected to income from digital products, it plays a crucial role in supporting a productive and efficient team that drives sales and innovation. Here's how HR software can benefit businesses selling digital products:

Benefits of HR Software for Digital Product Businesses

Talent Acquisition and Onboarding: Streamline the recruitment process by attracting top talent, managing applications, and onboarding new hires efficiently. This ensures you have the right people in place to develop, market, and sell your digital products effectively.

Performance Management and Development: Set clear goals for employees, track their progress, and provide feedback to optimize performance and encourage skill development. A skilled and motivated team can contribute significantly to creating high-quality digital products that resonate with your target audience.

Payroll and Benefits Management: Automate payroll processing, manage benefits administration, and ensure compliance with labor laws. This frees up valuable time for HR staff and minimizes payroll errors, allowing them to focus on strategic initiatives that support income generation.

Time and Attendance Tracking: Track employee hours accurately, especially if you have a remote workforce. This helps ensure fair compensation and facilitates data-driven decisions regarding staffing and project management.

Employee Self-Service: Empower employees to access paystubs, update personal information, request time off, and manage benefits through a self-service portal. This reduces administrative work for HR staff and improves employee satisfaction.

Specific Considerations for Digital Product Businesses:

Remote-Friendly Features: If your team is remote or geographically dispersed, choose software with features like video conferencing for interviews and onboarding, and collaboration tools for efficient project management.

Scalability: Consider how the software can accommodate your future growth plans. As your income from digital products increases and your team expands, the HR software should be able to handle the additional users and data.

Integrations: Choose software that integrates with other tools you use, such as accounting software for payroll processing or project management tools for tracking employee time on specific projects.

Popular HR Software for Digital Product Businesses:

Zenefits: A user-friendly platform with features like applicant tracking, onboarding, payroll, and benefits administration. Ideal for small and medium-sized businesses.

Gusto: An all-in-one HR platform offering payroll, benefits, expense management, and time tracking features.

BambooHR: Provides core HR functionalities like applicant tracking, onboarding, performance management, and self-service options.

Zoho People: A comprehensive HR suite with recruitment, onboarding, performance management, time tracking, and payroll functionalities.

Workday: A powerful solution for larger enterprises, offering advanced HR features like talent management, workforce analytics, and financial management.

Return on Investment (ROI):

Investing in HR software can improve your team's efficiency and productivity, leading to a higher quality product and potentially increased income. Additionally, it can help you attract and retain top talent, which is crucial for innovation and long-term success in the competitive digital product landscape.

Conclusion:
HR software plays a vital role in any business, but it's particularly important for those selling digital products. By optimizing your HR processes, you can empower your team to focus on creating and selling valuable products, ultimately maximizing your income from digital offerings. Remember, the right HR software can be a strategic investment that pays off in the long run.

22. Project Management Tools

The world of digital products thrives on efficient project management. From conceptualizing an idea to launching and iterating on your product, every step requires meticulous planning, collaboration, and resource allocation. Project management tools can be your secret weapon for maximizing income from digital products by streamlining workflows, boosting team productivity, and ensuring timely delivery.

Benefits of Project Management Tools for Digital Products:

Improved Organization and Planning: Break down complex digital product development projects into manageable tasks, track progress, and meet deadlines effectively.

Enhanced Team Collaboration: Facilitate communication and collaboration between team members working on different aspects of the product, fostering a unified effort.

Streamlined Workflows: Automate repetitive tasks and manage dependencies between tasks, ensuring a smooth flow of work throughout the development process.

Resource Management: Allocate resources efficiently, track team workload, and identify potential bottlenecks to optimize team capacity.

Centralized Communication: Consolidate communication in one platform, minimizing email clutter and ensuring everyone is on the same page.

Performance Tracking and Reporting: Monitor project progress, identify areas for improvement, and generate reports to gain insights and make data-driven decisions.

Features to Consider for Digital Product Teams:

Task Management: Create, assign, and track tasks with clear deadlines and dependencies.

Kanban Boards: Visualize project workflow with boards that display task status (e.g., To-Do, In Progress, Done).

File Sharing and Collaboration: Store and share files seamlessly within the platform, facilitating team collaboration on documents and resources.

Communication Tools: Integrate chat functionality or offer built-in messaging tools to foster real-time communication among team members.

Iteration and Version Control: Track changes, manage different versions of your product, and facilitate easy rollbacks if needed.

Integration with Design and Development Tools: Integrate seamlessly with design tools like Figma or development platforms like Git for a more connected and efficient workflow.

Popular Project Management Tools for Digital Products:

Asana: A user-friendly platform with strong task management, board view, and communication features.

Trello: A visual project management tool known for its Kanban boards and flexibility.

Monday.com: Highly customizable platform offering multiple project views, automation capabilities, and integrations.

Jira: Popular among software development teams, Jira excels in agile project management and bug tracking.

ClickUp: An all-in-one solution with task management, chat, time tracking, docs, and whiteboarding functionalities.

Choosing the Right Tool:

Team Size and Needs: Consider the size of your team, the complexity of your projects, and the specific features most relevant to your digital product development process.

Ease of Use: Evaluate the user interface and learning curve to ensure the chosen tool is user-friendly for your team.

Budget: Free and paid options are available, with paid tools offering more advanced features and integrations.

Scalability: Consider how the tool scales as your team and project complexity grow alongside your growing income from digital products.

Maximizing ROI with Project Management Tools:

Invest in training: Ensure your team understands how to use the tool effectively, maximizing its benefits.

Standardize workflows: Establish clear workflows within the project management tool to streamline collaboration.

Track progress and adapt: Regularly monitor project progress and use data insights to adjust plans and optimize your process.

Conclusion:
Project management tools are no longer a luxury, but rather a necessity for businesses selling digital products. By implementing the right tool and utilizing its features effectively, you can empower your team to be more productive, deliver high-quality products on time, and ultimately generate greater income from your digital offerings. Remember, the chosen tool should be an extension of your team, facilitating collaboration, streamlining workflows, and propelling your digital products towards success.

23. Advanced Customer Relationship Management (CRM) Systems

In the competitive digital product landscape, building strong customer relationships is paramount for maximizing income. Basic CRM systems can help manage customer data, but for businesses selling digital products, advanced CRM systems offer a deeper level of functionality to personalize the customer experience, boost sales, and cultivate long-term loyalty.

Benefits of Advanced CRMs for Digital Products:

Customer Segmentation and Targeting: Group customers based on demographics, purchase history, and behavior to deliver personalized marketing messages and product recommendations, leading to higher conversion rates and increased revenue.

Subscription Management: Manage recurring subscriptions effectively, automate renewal processes, and offer tiered subscription plans to cater to diverse customer needs. This can significantly increase customer lifetime value (CLTV) and recurring income.

Usage Analytics: Track user activity and analyze how customers interact with your digital product. These insights inform product development decisions, identify areas for improvement, and tailor features to enhance user engagement.

Customer Success Management: Proactively identify and address customer issues, offer targeted support, and guide users towards achieving their goals with your product. This fosters customer satisfaction, reduces churn, and increases the overall value proposition of your offerings.

Integration with Other Tools: Advanced CRMs integrate seamlessly with marketing automation tools, e-commerce platforms, and analytics software. This creates a centralized hub for managing customer data and interactions, improving overall efficiency.

AI-Powered Insights: Leverage artificial intelligence (AI) to gain deeper customer insights, predict customer behavior, and personalize recommendations based on individual preferences. This fosters a more engaging user experience and potentially fuels upselling and cross-selling opportunities.

Key Features for Digital Product Businesses:

Customer 360 View: Gain a holistic view of each customer, encompassing purchase history, support interactions, product usage data, and communication history.

Automated Workflows: Automate repetitive tasks like sending welcome emails, managing abandoned carts, or triggering renewal reminders for subscriptions.

Customer Self-Service Portal: Empower customers to manage their accounts, access resources, and troubleshoot issues independently through a self-service portal.

In-App Messaging: Offer real-time support within your digital product through chat functionalities, allowing for immediate engagement and resolution of customer queries.

Customer Loyalty Programs: Design and manage loyalty programs to reward repeat customers, incentivize product usage, and encourage upselling and cross-selling opportunities.

Examples of Advanced CRMs:

Salesforce Sales Cloud: A leading CRM platform offering comprehensive features for sales automation, customer management, and reporting.

Microsoft Dynamics 365 Customer Service: Focuses on customer service and support with features like case management, knowledge base, and live chat functionalities.

Zoho CRM: A robust, yet affordable CRM solution with features for sales, marketing, customer support, and analytics, catering to businesses of all sizes.

Freshsales: A user-friendly CRM known for its ease of use and features like conversation intelligence and gamification for sales teams.

Gainsight PX: Specifically designed for customer success management, offering features to onboard customers, track product usage, and proactively identify at-risk customers.

Choosing the Right Advanced CRM:

Business Needs: Evaluate your specific needs, team size, and budget to identify a platform with the functionality that best supports your digital product sales and customer management processes.

Scalability: Consider how the CRM can accommodate your future growth and adapt to your evolving customer base.

Integration Capabilities: Ensure the CRM integrates seamlessly with existing tools you use for marketing automation, e-commerce, or project management.

Conclusion:
Advanced CRMs are powerful tools for businesses selling digital products. By leveraging these features, you can gain a deeper understanding of your customers, personalize their experience, and build stronger relationships. Ultimately, advanced CRMs can be instrumental in driving sales, increasing customer retention, and maximizing your income from digital offerings. Remember, a well-implemented advanced CRM system is an investment that pays off in the long run, fostering customer loyalty and propelling your digital product business towards sustainable success.

24. Data Visualization Tools

In the world of digital products, data is king. Data about customer behavior, sales trends, and product usage holds the key to unlocking valuable insights that can help you optimize your offerings and maximize income. Data visualization tools transform raw data into clear, compelling visuals, enabling you to make informed decisions and track progress towards your financial goals.

Benefits of Data Visualization for Digital Products:

Identify Revenue Trends: Visualize sales data to identify trends, seasonal fluctuations, and top-performing products. This allows you to adjust marketing strategies, pricing models, and product development efforts to capitalize on profitable areas.

Understand Customer Behavior: Analyze user data to identify customer acquisition channels, purchase journeys, and engagement patterns. These insights help you personalize the customer experience, improve product features, and target marketing campaigns more effectively.

Track Marketing Performance: Visually represent campaign metrics like click-through rates, conversion rates, and customer acquisition costs. This helps you assess the effectiveness of your marketing efforts and optimize strategies for higher ROI.

Monitor Subscription Health: Track key metrics related to subscriptions, such as churn rate, average revenue per user (ARPU), and customer lifetime value (CLTV). Visualizing these metrics allows you to identify areas for improvement in your subscription model and implement strategies to retain subscribers.

Communicate Insights Clearly: Present complex data in a clear and concise format using dashboards, charts, and graphs. This enables you to share data insights with stakeholders, secure buy-in for new initiatives, and track progress towards revenue goals.

Popular Data Visualization Tools for Digital Products:

Free Tools:

Google Data Studio: A free tool from Google that integrates seamlessly with other Google products like Google Analytics and allows for easy data exploration and visualization.

Microsoft Power BI Desktop: Free for personal use, this tool offers robust data visualization capabilities and the ability to connect to various data sources.

Paid Tools:

Tableau: A leading platform for interactive data visualization, offering a wide range of chart types, customization options, and powerful data analysis features.

Looker: Focuses on business intelligence (BI) and data exploration, enabling users to create interactive dashboards and visualizations that can be embedded in applications or websites.

Domo: A cloud-based platform that combines data visualization, business intelligence, and enterprise performance management (EPM) capabilities.

Choosing the Right Tool:

Technical Expertise: Consider your team's data analysis skills and choose a tool with an appropriate learning curve.

Data Sources: Ensure the chosen tool can connect to the data sources you use, such as your CRM, marketing automation platform, or analytics software.

Data Volume and Complexity: If you work with large datasets or need advanced data analysis features, consider paid tools with more robust functionalities.

Collaboration and Sharing: Evaluate how easily you can share visualizations with stakeholders and collaborate with team members on data exploration.

Data Visualization Best Practices:

Focus on Clarity and Concision: Avoid cluttering visualizations with unnecessary information. Ensure charts are easy to understand and interpret for a wider audience.

Tell a Story with Data: Use data visualizations to highlight key insights and trends, guiding viewers towards actionable conclusions.

Interactive Visualizations: Consider using interactive dashboards or reports that allow users to explore data further and gain deeper understanding.

Visual Appeal Matters: Choose aesthetically pleasing charts and graphs that align with your brand identity and enhance the presentation of data.

Conclusion:
Data visualization tools are invaluable assets for businesses selling digital products. By transforming data into clear visuals, you can gain valuable insights into your customers, products, and

marketing efforts. These insights empower you to make data-driven decisions that optimize your offerings, generate higher sales, and ultimately maximize your income from digital products. Remember, data visualization is not just about creating beautiful charts; it's about using data to tell a compelling story of success and inform your path towards achieving your financial goals.

25. Gamified Learning Platforms

Gamified learning platforms have revolutionized education by incorporating game mechanics into the learning process. This engaging approach can be a powerful tool for generating income from digital products, particularly in the realm of online courses and educational resources. Here's how gamified learning platforms can boost your income:

Benefits of Gamified Learning for Revenue Generation:

Increased User Engagement: Game mechanics like points, badges, leaderboards, and challenges foster a more engaging learning experience. This keeps users motivated, promotes active participation, and increases course completion rates. Higher completion rates directly translate to higher potential revenue.

Improved Knowledge Retention: Gamification elements like interactive activities, quizzes, and rewards can enhance knowledge retention by making learning more fun and interactive. This leads to a higher perceived value of your learning content, justifying premium pricing models.

Subscription Model Opportunities: Gamified platforms can be well-suited for subscription models. Users can pay a monthly or annual fee for access to a library of gamified courses, continuously expanding their knowledge and earning rewards along the way.

Freemium Model with Upsells: Offer a basic level of content for free, using gamified features to entice users. Introduce premium content, such as advanced lessons or exclusive challenges, as paid add-ons, creating an opportunity for upselling within the platform.

Increased Customer Lifetime Value (CLTV): Engaged users who find your learning platform valuable are more likely to stick around and explore additional courses or features. This translates to a higher CLTV, allowing you to generate more revenue from each user over time.

Key Gamification Elements for Revenue Generation:

Points and Badges: Award points for completing lessons, participating in discussions, or achieving milestones. Offer badges as recognition for specific achievements, motivating users to strive for mastery.

Leaderboards: Create friendly competition by displaying user rankings based on points earned or challenges completed. This fosters a sense of community and encourages users to learn more to climb the leaderboard.

Levels and Progression: Introduce a leveling system with progressive difficulty. Users unlock new content, features, or challenges as they reach higher levels, promoting a sense of accomplishment and encouraging further learning.

Virtual Rewards: Offer virtual rewards like exclusive avatars, customization options, or in-game currency for completing tasks. These rewards incentivize further engagement and add an element of fun to the learning process.

Limited-Time Challenges: Introduce time-bound challenges related to specific topics within the course. Create a sense of urgency and motivate users to actively learn to complete the challenge within the timeframe.

Examples of Popular Gamified Learning Platforms:

Duolingo: A language learning platform that uses gamification elements like points, badges, leaderboards, and streaks to make language learning engaging and fun.

Memrise: Another language learning platform known for its gamified approach, focusing on spaced repetition and interactive activities to enhance memorization.

Udemy: Offers a mix of gamified and traditional courses. Some Udemy instructors utilize gamification elements like quizzes, challenges, and certificates of completion to create a more engaging learning experience.

Codecademy: Provides interactive coding tutorials and challenges that introduce programming concepts in a gamified format.

Kahoot!: A popular platform for creating gamified quizzes and educational games, ideal for K-12 education and classroom learning.

Considerations for Building a Revenue-Generating Gamified Platform:

Clearly Define Your Target Audience: Understanding your learners' needs and preferences allows you to tailor gamification elements for maximum engagement.

Balance Education and Fun: While gamification should be engaging, ensure the core learning objectives are not overshadowed by the fun elements.

Monitor User Behavior and Analytics: Track user engagement with gamification features and continuously adjust your approach based on user data and feedback.

Conclusion:
Gamified learning platforms offer a unique and effective way to generate income from digital products. By incorporating engaging game mechanics, you can boost user engagement, improve knowledge retention, and promote premium content or subscription models. Remember, the key lies in striking a balance between fun and education, while constantly adapting your approach based on user data and feedback. Gamified learning platforms can be a powerful tool for creating a lucrative and impactful educational experience.

26. Virtual Reality (VR) Training Simulations

Virtual Reality (VR) technology is rapidly transforming various industries, and the realm of training simulations is no exception. VR training offers immersive and interactive experiences that can revolutionize how employees learn and retain knowledge. This translates to a potential goldmine for businesses creating and selling VR training simulations as digital products.

Benefits of VR Training Simulations for Income Generation:

Premium Training Solutions: VR training offers a more engaging and effective alternative to traditional training methods. Businesses can charge premium prices for VR training simulations due to their immersive nature and the potential for improved learning outcomes.

Recurring Revenue Streams: Develop VR training simulations that cater to specific industry needs or job roles. Businesses can then offer these simulations as a subscription service, generating recurring revenue streams.

Scalability and Global Reach: VR training simulations are digital products. Once developed, they can be easily scaled and distributed globally, reaching a wider audience and maximizing potential income.

Reduced Training Costs: VR training can potentially reduce overall training costs by minimizing travel expenses for on-site training or eliminating the need for expensive physical training equipment.

Increased Employee Engagement: VR training is inherently engaging, leading to higher employee participation and potentially improving knowledge retention compared to traditional methods. This translates to a more skilled workforce and potentially higher productivity.

VR Training Applications with High Income Potential:

Safety Training: VR simulations can create realistic scenarios for safety training in hazardous environments, such as construction sites, manufacturing facilities, or aviation.

Soft Skills Training: Develop VR simulations for soft skills training, like communication, leadership, or conflict resolution. These simulations can provide employees with a safe and controlled environment to practice these skills.

Medical and Surgical Training: VR offers a unique platform for medical professionals to practice surgical procedures or complex medical scenarios in a realistic, risk-free environment.

Military Training: VR simulations can be used to train soldiers for combat situations, equipment familiarization, or practicing tactics in a virtual battlefield.

Customer Service Training: VR can help train customer service representatives by creating simulated customer interactions, allowing them to practice de-escalation techniques and problem-solving skills.

Considerations for Developing VR Training Simulations:

Target Audience and Needs: Clearly define your target audience and the specific training needs they have. This ensures the VR simulation is tailored for maximum effectiveness.

Development Cost and ROI: VR development can be expensive. Carefully assess development costs and projected income from sales or subscriptions to ensure a positive return on investment (ROI).

Technical Expertise: Developing VR training simulations may require specialized programming skills and a good understanding of VR development platforms.

Content Quality and Realism: Invest in high-quality graphics and realistic scenarios to create a truly immersive VR training experience.

Accessibility and Hardware Requirements: Consider the accessibility of your VR simulations. Will they require high-end VR headsets or be compatible with mobile VR solutions?

Examples of VR Training Success Stories:

Boeing: Uses VR simulations to train aircraft mechanics on assembly and maintenance procedures.

Walmart: Implemented VR training for store associates to practice customer service scenarios and emergency responses.

Medtronic: Develops VR simulations for surgeons to practice complex medical procedures on virtual patients.

Conclusion:
VR training simulations are a promising digital product with the potential for high income generation. By understanding the training needs of specific industries, developing engaging and effective VR simulations, and ensuring accessibility, businesses can capitalize on this growing market. VR training offers a win-win scenario for both creators and users, providing immersive learning

experiences and a path towards a more skilled and prepared workforce. As VR technology continues to evolve and become more affordable, expect to see VR training simulations becoming a mainstay in various industries, generating significant revenue for those at the forefront of this exciting digital frontier.

27. Advanced Online Courses with Personalized Learning Paths

The online course market is booming, but competition is fierce. To stand out and maximize income, consider offering advanced online courses with personalized learning paths. This approach caters to individual needs and learning styles, leading to higher engagement, completion rates, and ultimately, greater revenue for your digital product.

Benefits of Personalized Learning Paths for Income Generation:

Increased Course Completion Rates: Personalized learning paths cater to individual learning styles and goals, making the learning process more engaging and relevant. This translates to higher completion rates, leading to more satisfied customers and potentially increased revenue per course.

Premium Pricing Justification: The ability to offer a customized learning experience allows you to justify premium pricing for your advanced courses. Learners are more likely to pay a higher price for a course that caters to their specific needs and helps them achieve their desired learning outcomes.

Reduced Customer Churn: Personalized learning reduces the frustration of irrelevant content and keeps learners engaged. This fosters customer satisfaction and loyalty, reducing churn and encouraging repeat business through additional course purchases.

Upselling and Cross-Selling Opportunities: Personalized learning paths can identify a learner's knowledge gaps and suggest additional courses or resources that fill those gaps. This creates upselling and cross-selling opportunities within your course catalog, increasing your revenue potential.

Improved Brand Reputation: A focus on personalized learning signifies a commitment to quality education and student success. This can enhance your brand reputation and attract more learners, leading to higher income in the long run.

Key Features for Personalized Learning:

Assessments and Learning Style Identification: Offer pre-course assessments to gauge learners' prior knowledge and learning style preferences (e.g., visual, auditory, kinesthetic).

Adaptive Learning Technology: Implement technology that adjusts course content and delivery based on a learner's progress and performance. This ensures learners are challenged appropriately and don't waste time on material they already know.

Branched Learning Paths: Create multiple learning paths within your course, allowing learners to choose modules or activities that align with their specific goals and needs.

Curated Content Recommendations: Based on learning progress and assessments, suggest additional resources, articles, or videos to deepen understanding of specific topics.

Progress Tracking and Feedback: Provide learners with tools to track their progress, identify areas for improvement, and receive personalized feedback throughout the course.

Examples of Platforms Supporting Personalized Learning:

Thinkific: Offers features like quizzes, assignments, and course completion certificates, allowing for personalized course structures.

Teachable: Provides basic personalization functionalities, including course customization options and drip content delivery based on schedules.

Kajabi: A platform with tools for creating personalized learning paths, progress tracking, and student communities for enhanced interaction.

Udemy: While not as advanced, some Udemy instructors utilize quizzes and branching scenarios within their courses to create a more personalized experience.

Podia: Provides features for personalized learning paths, memberships, and drip content delivery, allowing for a tailored learning experience.

Developing Effective Personalized Learning Paths:

Identify Learning Objectives: Clearly define the key learning outcomes for your course and how personalized paths will help achieve them.

Segment Your Audience: Group learners based on their learning styles, prior knowledge, and desired outcomes.

Content Chunks and Assessments: Create modular content and assessments that cater to different learning needs and allow for branching pathways based on performance.

Continuous Improvement: Track student engagement with personalized paths and gather feedback to refine and optimize your approach.

Conclusion:
Advanced online courses with personalized learning paths are not just a trend; they are a strategic approach to maximizing income in the online learning space. By catering to individual learners and offering a customized learning experience, you can increase course completion rates, justify premium pricing, and build a loyal customer base. Remember, personalized learning shows a commitment to student success, ultimately leading to a thriving online course business and a stronger brand reputation in the competitive online learning market.

28. Language Learning Apps with AI-Powered Chatbots

Language learning apps have become a popular way for people to learn on the go. However, the market is crowded, and standing out requires innovative features. AI-powered chatbots can be your secret weapon, transforming language learning apps into engaging conversational experiences that drive user engagement and ultimately, revenue growth.

Benefits of AI Chatbots in Language Learning Apps:

Personalized Learning: Chatbots can adapt conversations based on a user's learning level, interests, and mistakes. This personalized approach keeps users engaged and motivated to learn.

Simulated Conversations: Chatbots provide a safe space for users to practice speaking and listening in a real-world context. This improves confidence and fluency in everyday conversations.

24/7 Availability: Unlike human tutors, chatbots are available 24/7. Learners can practice anytime, anywhere, fitting their language learning into their busy schedules.

Gamification and Motivation: Chatbots can be gamified by incorporating points, badges, and challenges within conversations. This adds a fun element and motivates users to keep learning.

Targeted Feedback and Error Correction: AI chatbots can identify and correct user mistakes in real-time, providing immediate feedback without judgment.

Data-Driven Insights: Chatbots track user interactions and progress, providing valuable data on learning patterns and areas for improvement. This allows you to refine your app and personalize the learning experience further.

Specific Considerations for Digital Product Businesses:

Freemium Model: Offer a basic level of the app for free, including chatbot interactions with limited topics or functionalities. Introduce premium features like advanced conversation topics, personalized feedback reports, or vocabulary builders as paid upgrades.

Subscription Model: Provide access to the full range of chatbot functionalities and conversation topics through a monthly or annual subscription.

This creates a recurring revenue stream and incentivizes continued learning.

In-App Purchases: Offer additional features within the app, such as personalized lesson plans or access to native speaker voice packs for the chatbot, as in-app purchases.

Targeted Advertising: Leverage user data collected through chatbot interactions to deliver targeted in-app advertisements for relevant language learning resources or cultural experiences.

Developing Effective AI Chatbots for Language Learning:

Natural Language Processing (NLP): Ensure your chatbot utilizes NLP to understand user input and respond with grammatically correct and contextually relevant language.

Voice Recognition and Text-to-Speech: Integrate voice recognition for spoken conversation practice and text-to-speech functionality for realistic chatbot responses.

Personality and Engagement: Design your chatbot with a personality that resonates with your target audience and encourages engaging conversations.

Continuous Learning and Improvement: Train your chatbot with a vast dataset of conversations and user interactions. This allows it to learn and adapt over time, providing a more natural and effective learning experience.

Examples of Language Learning Apps with AI Chatbots:

Duolingo: Offers a chatbot feature called "Duolingo Bots" for practicing conversation skills on specific topics.

Babbel: Provides interactive dialogues voiced by native speakers, simulating real-life conversations.

MosaLingua: Integrates a chatbot function for practicing vocabulary and grammar through interactive dialogues.

Mondly: Offers chatbot conversations with a focus on pronunciation and fluency practice.

Elsa Speak: Utilizes AI to analyze pronunciation and offer personalized feedback through a virtual conversation partner.

Language learning apps with AI-powered chatbots offer a unique and engaging way for people to learn languages. By providing personalized learning experiences, simulated conversations, and real-time feedback, these apps can significantly improve user engagement, leading to increased revenue through various monetization strategies.

29. Augmented Reality (AR) Filters

Augmented reality (AR) filters have exploded in popularity on social media platforms like Instagram, Snapchat, and Facebook. These interactive filters overlay digital elements onto the real world, creating playful and engaging experiences for users. But beyond the fun factor, AR filters present a lucrative opportunity to generate income from digital products.

Benefits of AR Filters for Revenue Generation:

Branded AR Experiences: Partner with businesses to create branded AR filters that promote products, services, or special offers. Users can virtually try on makeup, visualize furniture in their homes, or interact with branded elements within the filter. This creates a unique and engaging marketing experience with high brand recall.

In-App Purchases: Develop AR filters with unlockable features or downloadable content within the app. Users can pay to access additional effects, animations, or customization options for their AR experience.

Freemium Model: Offer a basic set of AR filters for free and introduce premium filters with more advanced features or effects as paid downloads.

Subscription Model: Provide access to a library of exclusive AR filters through a monthly or annual subscription. This creates a recurring revenue stream and incentivizes users to explore a wider variety of filters.

Data Insights and Targeted Advertising: Track user engagement with AR filters and gather anonymized data on preferences and demographics. This data can be used to create more targeted advertising campaigns or inform future AR filter development based on user trends.

Monetization Strategies for AR Filters:

Direct Sales: Develop custom AR filters for brands and businesses for a one-time fee.

Affiliate Marketing: Partner with brands and include affiliate links within your AR filters. Users who click the link and make a purchase generate revenue for you.

Sponsored Filters: Collaborate with brands to create sponsored AR filters that promote their products or services prominently within the filter experience.

Developing Engaging AR Filters for Revenue:

Focus on User Experience: Design AR filters that are fun, interactive, and offer a unique value proposition for users. Ensure the filters are easy to use and visually appealing.

Leverage Social Media Integration: Develop AR filters that are specifically designed for popular social media platforms to reach a wider audience and encourage user-generated content with your filter.

Track User Engagement and Analytics: Monitor how users interact with your AR filters and analyze data to understand user preferences and identify areas for improvement.

Stay Updated on Trends: Keep an eye on emerging trends in AR technology and social media and adapt your filter designs to stay relevant and engaging.

Examples of AR Filters Used for Revenue Generation:

Sephora: Offers AR filters that allow users to virtually try on makeup before purchase.

Warby Parker: Developed AR filters for users to virtually try on different eyeglasses frames.

Nike: Created AR filters that showcase new sneaker releases with interactive features.

Gucci: Partnered with Snapchat to create an AR filter for a virtual try-on experience with their new shoe line.

NBA: Offered AR filters that allowed fans to virtually interact with their favorite teams and players.

Conclusion:
AR filters are a powerful tool for creating engaging digital products with significant income potential. By focusing on user experience, collaborating with brands, and utilizing effective monetization strategies, you can capitalize on this booming market. Remember, the key lies in developing innovative and interactive AR filters that provide value to both users and brands, ultimately propelling your digital product business towards sustainable growth.

30. High-Fidelity Mockups & Prototypes

In the competitive world of digital products, first impressions matter. High-fidelity mockups and prototypes are not just design deliverables; they are powerful tools that can significantly impact the success of your digital product and ultimately, your income. Here's how investing in high-fidelity mockups and prototypes can pave the way for increased revenue:

Benefits of High-Fidelity Mockups & Prototypes for Revenue Generation:

Improved Stakeholder Communication: High-fidelity mockups provide a clear and realistic visual representation of your product, fostering better communication with stakeholders like investors, clients, or team members. This reduces the risk of misunderstandings and ensures everyone is on the same page from the outset.

Early User Feedback: Interactive prototypes allow you to gather valuable user feedback early in the development process. This feedback can identify usability issues, suggest improvements to features, and validate product concepts before significant development resources are invested. This can save time and money in the long run, leading to a more successful product launch.

Investor Confidence: High-fidelity mockups and prototypes demonstrate the professionalism and attention to detail behind your digital product. This can inspire greater confidence in potential investors, making it easier to secure funding for product development.

Reduced Development Costs: Identifying and addressing usability issues early through user testing with prototypes can prevent costly rework later in the development process. This translates to a more efficient development cycle and potentially lower overall costs.

Enhanced User Experience: By incorporating user feedback from prototypes, you can ensure your final product delivers a smooth, intuitive, and enjoyable user experience. This translates to higher user satisfaction and engagement, ultimately leading to higher revenue potential.

Key Features of High-Fidelity Mockups & Prototypes:

High-Quality Visuals: Mockups should look polished and realistic, with clear graphics, fonts, and design elements that reflect your brand identity.

Interactive Elements: Prototypes should allow users to interact with core functionalities and navigate through key user flows. This provides a realistic experience and valuable insights into usability.

Realistic Data and Content: Use realistic data and content within prototypes to accurately simulate the final product experience.

Microinteractions: Incorporate subtle animations and effects that mimic real-world interactions with the product to enhance user engagement.

Accessibility Considerations: Ensure your mockups and prototypes adhere to accessibility guidelines to cater to users with disabilities, creating a more inclusive product.

Tools for Creating High-Fidelity Mockups & Prototypes:

Figma: A popular design tool with features for creating both static mockups and interactive prototypes.

Adobe XD: Offers a comprehensive solution for user experience (UX) design, including high-fidelity mockup and prototyping functionalities.

InVision: Focuses specifically on prototyping, allowing for the creation of highly interactive prototypes with advanced features.

Sketch: A vector graphics editor known for its user-friendly interface and strong capabilities for creating high-quality mockups.

Proto.io: Another popular prototyping tool known for its ease of use and ability to create web, mobile, and desktop app prototypes.

Investing Wisely in High-Fidelity Mockups & Prototypes:

Prioritize Core Features: Focus on creating high-fidelity mockups and prototypes for the core functionalities of your product first.

Tailor the Level of Fidelity: Consider the stage of development and the needs of your stakeholders. Early mockups may not need to be as detailed as prototypes used for user testing.

Conduct User Testing Effectively: Plan user testing sessions with clear objectives and recruit participants that represent your target audience. Analyze feedback carefully and iterate on your designs based on insights.

Conclusion:
Investing in high-fidelity mockups and prototypes is not an expense; it's an investment in the future success of your digital product. By providing clarity,

facilitating early feedback, and ensuring user experience is prioritized, these tools can play a crucial role in maximizing your income potential. Remember, high-fidelity mockups and prototypes are a bridge between your vision and a successful product launch, leading to a digital offering that resonates with users and generates sustainable revenue.

31. Machine Learning Algorithms

Machine learning (ML) algorithms are transforming the digital product landscape. By leveraging vast amounts of data, these algorithms can uncover hidden patterns, personalize experiences, and optimize decision-making, ultimately leading to significant revenue growth for your digital product. Here's how machine learning empowers income generation:

Benefits of Machine Learning for Digital Products:

Personalized Recommendations: ML algorithms analyze user data to recommend products, content, or features most relevant to their interests and past behavior. This targeted approach increases conversion rates and in-app purchases.

Dynamic Pricing Models: Implement algorithms to set dynamic pricing strategies based on factors like user behavior, market trends, and competitor pricing. This maximizes revenue potential while optimizing customer value.

Fraud Detection and Prevention: ML algorithms can analyze user activity and identify patterns indicative of fraudulent transactions. This protects your business from financial losses and maintains customer trust.

Churn Prediction and Customer Retention: Identify users at risk of churn by analyzing usage patterns and user data. Develop targeted campaigns to win back at-risk customers and improve customer lifetime value (CLTV).

Content Optimization and A/B Testing: ML algorithms can automate A/B testing and content optimization processes. This allows you to identify the most effective design elements and content variations that drive higher engagement and conversions.

Improved Search Functionality: Develop intelligent search features powered by ML that understand user intent and deliver highly relevant search results. This enhances user experience and increases the likelihood of users finding the products or content they are looking for.

Machine Learning Algorithms for Specific Revenue Streams:

Subscription Model: Predict churn risk and personalize subscription offers to retain subscribers and maximize recurring revenue.

Freemium Model: Use ML to identify high-value free users and recommend premium features or upgrades that convert them into paying customers.

In-App Purchases: Recommend relevant in-app purchases based on user behavior and context, increasing the likelihood of users spending money within your app.

Targeted Advertising: Leverage ML to deliver highly targeted advertising within your app or digital product, generating revenue from ad impressions or clicks.

Examples of Machine Learning Applications in Digital Products:

Netflix: Recommends movies and shows based on a user's watch history and viewing preferences.

Amazon: Uses ML for personalized product recommendations, dynamic pricing strategies, and targeted advertising.

Spotify: Creates personalized playlists and music recommendations based on user listening habits.

Uber: Optimizes pricing based on factors like demand, location, and historical data to maximize revenue while keeping wait times low.

Airbnb: Recommends personalized listings and optimizes pricing for hosts to maximize bookings and revenue.

Considerations for Implementing Machine Learning:

Data Quality and Security: Ensure the data used to train your ML models is high-quality, clean, and secure to avoid biased or inaccurate results.

Model Selection and Training: Choose appropriate ML algorithms for your specific goals and ensure they are properly trained on a representative dataset.

Model Explainability and Transparency: Understand how your ML models arrive at their recommendations or decisions to ensure fairness and avoid unintended bias.

Continuous Monitoring and Improvement: Continuously monitor your ML models and retrain them with new data to ensure they remain effective and adapt to evolving user behavior.

Conclusion:
Machine learning algorithms are not just a technological marvel; they are a powerful tool for driving revenue growth in the digital product space. By implementing ML algorithms strategically, you can personalize user experiences, optimize pricing

models, and predict customer behavior. This translates to increased customer satisfaction, higher conversion rates, and a thriving digital product business. Remember, successful ML implementation requires careful planning, high-quality data, and ongoing monitoring to ensure your algorithms are working for you and ultimately propelling your digital product towards long-term financial success.

32. Cybersecurity Tools

The digital landscape offers a fantastic opportunity to generate income through various products like ebooks, online courses, software, and templates. However, protecting your intellectual property and customer data is crucial for sustainable success. This is where cybersecurity tools come in.

Here's a detailed breakdown of how cybersecurity tools can safeguard your income from digital products:

1. Content Protection:

Digital Rights Management (DRM): DRM solutions encrypt your digital products, restricting unauthorized access and duplication. This ensures customers pay for what they get and discourages piracy.

Password Protection: Password-protect specific sections of your digital products or require passwords for access. This adds a layer of security for premium content or sensitive information.

2. Secure Delivery Platforms:

Ecommerce platforms: Utilize secure platforms like Shopify or Gumroad for selling your digital products. These platforms handle transactions securely and offer built-in customer data protection.

Cloud Storage: Consider storing your digital products on secure cloud storage services like Dropbox or Google Drive. These services offer access controls and encryption, preventing unauthorized access.

3. Customer Data Protection:

Payment Gateways: Integrate secure payment gateways like PayPal or Stripe for processing customer transactions. These gateways ensure PCI compliance and protect sensitive financial data.

Customer Relationship Management (CRM) Systems: Utilize CRM systems to manage customer data securely. These systems offer access control and data encryption, minimizing the risk of breaches.

4. Website Security:

Secure Sockets Layer (SSL) Certificates: Implement SSL certificates on your website to encrypt communication between your server and customer browsers. This safeguards sensitive data like credit card information.

Website Security Scans: Regularly conduct website security scans to identify vulnerabilities hackers might exploit. These scans help proactively address security weaknesses.

5. Backup and Disaster Recovery:

Regular Backups: Regularly back up your digital products and customer data to a secure location. This ensures you have a copy in case of system failures or cyberattacks.

Disaster Recovery Plan: Develop a disaster recovery plan outlining steps to recover your data and website in case of a cyberattack or natural disaster.

Additional Considerations:

Strong Passwords: Enforce strong password policies for customer accounts and your own administrative access.

Security Awareness Training: Educate yourself and your team on cybersecurity best practices to identify and avoid phishing attempts and other social engineering tactics.

Stay Updated: Keep your software and security tools updated with the latest patches to address vulnerabilities discovered by security researchers.

By implementing these cybersecurity tools and strategies, you can create a secure environment for your digital products, fostering trust with your customers and protecting your income stream.

Remember, cybersecurity is an ongoing process, so stay vigilant and adapt your approach as the digital landscape evolves.

33. Custom Content Management Systems (CMS)

In the world of digital products, content is king. But managing and delivering that content efficiently can be a challenge, especially as your product offerings grow. This is where Custom Content Management Systems (CMS) come into play.

A Custom CMS is a software application built specifically for your needs, allowing you to manage and deliver the content behind your digital products. Here's how a Custom CMS can empower you to maximize income from digital products:

Enhanced User Experience:

Streamlined Content Delivery: A Custom CMS lets you tailor the user experience for different products. You can create dedicated sections for ebooks, course materials, software documentation, or any other digital offering, making it easy for users to find what they need.

Personalized Content: Personalize content delivery based on user subscriptions, purchase history, or preferences. This allows you to offer tiered access or upsell additional products based on user engagement.

Improved Sales and Marketing:

Efficient Product Updates: Easily update and add new features or content to existing digital products. This allows you to maintain product freshness and incentivize repeat purchases.

Content Marketing Integration: Tightly integrate your CMS with marketing tools for content promotion and lead generation. You can create landing pages, manage blog posts, and distribute product updates seamlessly.

Scalability and Security:

Future-proof Growth: A Custom CMS can be built to scale with your business. As your product offerings expand, the CMS can adapt to handle the increased content management needs.

Enhanced Security: Custom CMS solutions offer greater control over user access and data security compared to generic platforms. This is crucial for protecting sensitive product information and customer data.

Additional Considerations:
Development Cost: Building a Custom CMS can be expensive compared to off-the-shelf solutions. Weigh the development cost against the long-term benefits for your specific business needs.

Technical Expertise: Managing a Custom CMS often requires technical expertise. Consider ongoing maintenance costs or hiring dedicated personnel if needed.

Integration Flexibility: Ensure your Custom CMS can integrate with existing tools and services you use for sales, marketing, and customer support for a smooth workflow.

Who can benefit from a Custom CMS?

Custom CMS solutions are ideal for businesses with complex digital product offerings, a large user base, or a strong focus on content personalization. For example, if you sell online courses with various learning modules, subscriptions with tiered access levels, or software with extensive documentation, a Custom CMS can streamline content management and improve user experience significantly.

While off-the-shelf CMS options exist, a Custom CMS offers a powerful and scalable solution for managing and delivering content that fuels sales of your digital products. By carefully evaluating your needs and resources, a Custom CMS can be a valuable investment that boosts your income potential.

34. Advanced Online Courses with Personalized Learning Paths

The online learning landscape is evolving, with a growing demand for in-depth, personalized learning experiences. Advanced online courses with personalized learning paths cater to this need, offering a compelling digital product for knowledge-hungry learners. This detailed note explores how to leverage this trend and generate income by creating exceptional educational experiences.

The Power of Personalization

Traditional online courses often follow a one-size-fits-all approach. Personalized learning paths address this limitation by:

Assessing Individual Needs: Diagnostic tools or quizzes determine a student's current knowledge level and learning goals.

Curated Content: Learning paths recommend specific modules, resources, and activities based on individual assessments.

Adaptive Learning: Advanced platforms adjust the difficulty level and content sequence based on a student's progress.

Enhanced Engagement: Personalized experiences keep learners motivated and focused on achieving their goals.

Developing Profitable Advanced Online Courses

Content Expertise: Establish yourself as a subject matter expert in a niche field with high earning potential (coding, data science, marketing).

Course Structure: Break down your subject into well-organized modules with clear learning objectives.

High-Quality Production: Invest in professional video production, engaging visuals, and interactive elements for optimal learning.

Assessment Strategies: Integrate quizzes, assignments, and projects to gauge student understanding and tailor the learning path accordingly.

Personalized Learning Path Strategies

Interactive Assessments: Develop engaging quizzes and surveys to pinpoint a student's strengths and weaknesses.

Branching Learning Paths: Offer different content modules and activities based on assessment results.

Adaptive Delivery: Utilize learning management systems (LMS) with adaptive learning functionalities.

Expert Feedback & Coaching: Provide personalized feedback on assignments and offer optional coaching sessions for deeper learning.

Monetization Strategies

Premium Course Access: Offer tiered pricing with access to personalized learning paths as a premium feature.

Subscription Model: Provide access to a library of advanced courses with personalized learning paths for a monthly or annual fee.

Certificate Programs: Award completion certificates upon successful completion of personalized learning paths for increased value.

Additional Considerations

Market Research: Identify in-demand skills and knowledge gaps in your chosen niche to ensure course relevance.

Community Building: Foster a community forum or online platform for students to ask questions, share experiences, and network.

Technological Expertise: Invest in a robust LMS platform that supports personalized learning path functionalities.

Content Updates: Keep course content and assessments current with industry trends and advancements.

Conclusion
Advanced online courses with personalized learning paths offer a lucrative opportunity to create high-value digital products. By establishing expertise in a profitable niche, crafting engaging content, and implementing personalized learning strategies, you can revolutionize online education and build a thriving business that empowers learners to achieve their full potential.

35. Big Data Analytics Platforms

The success of any digital product hinges on understanding your customers and their behavior. Big data analytics platforms can be powerful tools for extracting valuable insights from the vast amount of data generated by your digital products. Here's how big data analytics can boost your income from digital products:

Unveiling Customer Behavior:

User Engagement: Analyze user behavior within your digital products. Identify popular features, content sections with low engagement, and areas for improvement. This allows you to optimize your products for better user experience and potentially increase sales.

Customer Segmentation: Segment your customer base based on demographics, purchase history, and usage patterns. This enables you to personalize marketing campaigns, offer targeted product recommendations, and develop upsell or cross-sell strategies.

Predictive Analytics: Leverage big data to predict customer churn and identify at-risk users. This allows you to implement proactive retention strategies and potentially save valuable recurring revenue.

Boosting Product Development:

Market Trends: Analyze market trends and competitor data to identify new opportunities and develop innovative digital products that cater to evolving customer needs.

A/B Testing: Conduct A/B testing on different features, pricing models, or marketing messages. Big data analytics helps you measure the impact of these variations and choose the options that drive higher conversions and revenue.

Product Innovation: Identify usage patterns that reveal unmet customer needs. This can guide product development efforts towards features and functionalities that enhance product value and encourage repeat purchases.

Maximizing Marketing ROI:

Targeted Advertising: Utilize customer insights to personalize and target your advertising campaigns. This ensures your marketing efforts reach the right audience, leading to higher conversion rates and a better return on investment.

Content Optimization: Analyze content performance data to understand what resonates with your audience. This helps you create targeted content that drives engagement and potentially leads to higher product sales.

Pricing Optimization: Analyze user behavior and subscription patterns to determine optimal pricing strategies. This could involve introducing tiered subscription models, offering discounts, or adjusting pricing based on market trends.

Choosing the Right Big Data Platform:

Several big data analytics platforms cater to businesses of all sizes. Here are some factors to consider when choosing a platform:

Data Volume: Consider the volume of data your digital product generates. Choose a platform that can handle your current data needs and scales as your business grows.

Ease of Use: Evaluate the platform's user interface and any required technical expertise. Look for solutions that offer intuitive dashboards and reports, even if you don't have a dedicated data science team.

Cost: Big data platforms can come with varying pricing structures. Explore options that fit your budget and consider the potential return on investment the platform can offer.

The Takeaway:

Big data analytics platforms offer a goldmine of insights for businesses selling digital products. By understanding your customers, optimizing your products, and fine-tuning your marketing strategies, big data can be a powerful tool for maximizing your income potential. Carefully evaluate your needs and resources to choose the right platform that unlocks the hidden potential within your digital product data.

36. Interactive simulations for complex systems

The world of digital products is vast, but there's a unique niche where interactive simulations for complex systems can be a powerful tool for generating income. Here's how:

Targeted Audience:

Educational Tools: Develop interactive simulations for educational purposes. These could target students in science, engineering, economics, or any field where understanding complex systems is crucial. Imagine simulations of weather patterns, stock market behavior, or the spread of infectious diseases.

Training and Professional Development: Create interactive simulations for professional training in various industries. For example, pilot training simulators, financial modeling simulations, or simulations for medical professionals practicing complex procedures.

Gamification for Learning: Infuse gamification elements into your simulations to make learning engaging and interactive. This can attract a wider audience and increase user retention, leading to potential subscription models or recurring revenue.

Monetization Strategies:

Subscription Model: Offer tiered subscription plans for access to your simulations. Basic plans could provide limited functionality, while premium plans offer advanced features, customization options, or access to a wider range of simulations.

Freemium Model: Provide a free basic version of your simulation with limited functionality. This can attract users and showcase the value proposition. Paid upgrades can unlock advanced features, in-depth analysis tools, or access to exclusive content within the simulation.

Licensing for Educational Institutions: Develop licensing models for schools, universities, or training institutes to integrate your simulations into their curriculum or training programs.

Consulting and Customization: Offer additional services like customizing simulations for specific needs or providing consulting services on using your simulations for training or research purposes.

Benefits and Considerations:

High-Value Niche: Interactive simulations for complex systems cater to a specific audience with a strong need for this type of learning tool. This can potentially command a premium price compared to more generic digital products.

Recurring Revenue: Subscription models or tiered pricing structures can provide a steady stream of income, making your digital product business more sustainable.

Technical Expertise: Developing interactive simulations often requires specialized programming skills and a good understanding of the complex systems being modeled.

The Takeaway:

Interactive simulations for complex systems offer a unique and potentially lucrative niche within the digital product landscape. Carefully choose your target audience, develop engaging and informative simulations, and explore various monetization strategies to build a sustainable income stream. Remember, the technical expertise needed for development can be a barrier, so assess your resources and consider collaborating with developers to bring your simulations to life.

37. Adaptive Learning Platforms that tailor content to individual student needs

In the competitive world of online education, personalization is key. Adaptive learning platforms that tailor content to individual student needs offer a powerful advantage and can be a significant source of income from digital products.Here's how:

Benefits of Adaptive Learning:

Improved Learning Outcomes: By adapting to each student's strengths and weaknesses, adaptive platforms ensure a more efficient learning experience. Students spend less time on topics they already grasp and focus on areas needing improvement, leading to higher knowledge retention and better overall learning outcomes.

Increased Student Engagement: Personalized learning keeps students engaged. The platform caters to their individual pace and learning style, making the learning process more dynamic and interesting. Higher engagement translates to increased course completion rates and potentially higher customer satisfaction.

Differentiation in a Crowded Market: Adaptive learning platforms offer a unique value proposition compared to traditional online courses. By catering to individual needs, you stand out from the competition, potentially attracting a wider student base and driving higher sales for your digital product.

Monetization Strategies:

Subscription Model: Offer tiered subscriptions based on access levels. Basic plans could provide access to a limited number of courses or features, while premium plans offer access to all courses, personalized learning paths, or advanced analytics for students.

Course Bundles: Create targeted course bundles that address specific learning objectives or skill sets. This allows students to choose the most relevant content and provides you with an opportunity to upsell additional courses.

Micro-learning Modules: Develop shorter, focused learning modules on specific topics within a broader subject area. This allows students to purchase individual modules based on their specific needs, generating additional revenue streams.

Institutional Licensing: Offer licensing models for schools, universities, or training institutions to integrate your adaptive learning platform into their curriculum. This can be a lucrative way to expand your reach and generate recurring revenue.

Additional Considerations:

Content Development: Developing high-quality, adaptive learning content requires expertise in the subject matter and an understanding of adaptive learning principles. Consider involving subject matter experts and instructional designers in the development process.

Data Security and Privacy: Student data privacy is paramount. Ensure your platform complies with data security regulations and provides transparent data collection and usage practices.

Scalability: As your platform grows and attracts more users, ensure it can scale efficiently to handle the increased traffic and data volume.

The Takeaway:

Adaptive learning platforms represent a compelling approach to online education, offering a personalized learning experience that benefits students and boosts income potential. By focusing on quality content, diverse monetization strategies, and secure data practices, you can create a successful digital product that stands out in the online learning market.

38. Stock Market Prediction Models

While the allure of leveraging stock market predictions for digital products is understandable, it's important to approach this concept with caution. Here's why:

Market Uncertainty:

Unpredictable Nature: The stock market is inherently complex and influenced by a multitude of unforeseen factors. Economic events, political instability, and even social media trends can significantly impact stock prices, making accurate predictions extremely challenging.

Historical Data Limitations: Prediction models rely on historical data to identify patterns and trends. However, past performance is not always indicative of future results. Relying solely on historical data can lead to inaccurate predictions.

Legal and Ethical Considerations:

Financial Regulations: Selling financial advice or recommendations based on your predictions might fall under financial regulations. Ensure you comply with relevant licensing and disclosure requirements to avoid legal issues.

Misleading Information: Even with the best intentions, inaccurate predictions can lead to financial losses for your users. Be transparent about the limitations of your models and avoid making absolute claims about future market performance.

Alternative Approaches for Digital Products:

Educational Tools: Develop educational tools that teach users about stock market fundamentals, technical analysis, and investment strategies. This empowers users to make informed decisions rather than relying solely on predictions.

Market Analysis and Insights: Offer market analysis reports, news feeds, and expert commentary to help users stay informed about current market trends and make their own investment choices.

Portfolio Management Tools: Create digital products that assist users with portfolio management, diversification strategies, and risk assessment. This empowers users to build and manage their investments based on their individual goals and risk tolerance.

While stock market prediction models might seem like a tempting proposition for digital products, the inherent uncertainty of the market and potential legal and ethical concerns make it a risky approach. Consider alternative digital products that focus on financial education, market analysis tools, or portfolio management to provide valuable resources for your users without venturing into the realm of uncertain predictions. By focusing on empowering users with knowledge and tools, you can build a more sustainable and responsible digital product business in the financial space.

39. 3D-printable object designs

The world of 3D printing has opened up exciting possibilities for creating and selling digital products. 3D-printable object designs offer a unique and potentially lucrative niche within the digital product landscape. Here's a breakdown of how you can leverage 3D-printable object designs to generate income:

Target Audience:

Hobbyists and Makers: A large community of hobbyists and makers have embraced 3D printing. Offer designs for figurines, functional objects, customizable tools, or decorative pieces that cater to their interests.

Educators and Students: Design educational models for STEM learning, historical replicas, or anatomical models for use in classrooms or personal projects.

Entrepreneurs and Businesses: Create printable designs for functional prototypes, marketing materials, custom packaging, or even replacement parts for existing products.

Monetization Strategies:

Sell Individual Designs: Sell your designs individually on online marketplaces like Etsy, Cults3D, or CGTrader. These platforms connect you with a global audience of potential buyers interested in 3D printing your designs.

Subscription Model: Offer a subscription service where users pay a monthly fee for access to a library of your designs. This can be a good option if you have a large and diverse collection of designs.

Freemium Model: Provide a limited selection of free designs to showcase your work and entice users to purchase more complex or premium designs.

Customization Services: Offer customization options on your designs. This could involve allowing users to personalize the size, color, or add inscriptions to your models before purchasing the printable file.

Design Considerations:

Printability: Ensure your designs are optimized for 3D printing. Consider factors like overhangs, wall thickness, and support structures to create models that print successfully on various 3D printers.

Variety and Niche Focus: Offer a range of designs that cater to different interests and needs. You can also focus on a specific niche, like gaming miniatures, functional household items, or educational models, to establish yourself as a go-to source for that category.

Target Audience Expertise: Tailor the complexity of your designs to your target audience. For beginners, offer easy-to-print models with clear instructions. For experienced makers, provide more intricate designs with advanced features.

Additional Tips:

Marketing and Branding: Build a strong online presence showcasing your designs. Utilize social media platforms like Instagram or Pinterest to visually promote your work and engage with potential customers.

Community Engagement: Participate in online forums and communities dedicated to 3D printing. This allows you to connect with potential customers, get feedback on your designs, and stay updated on current trends in the 3D printing world.

Legal Considerations: Be mindful of copyright and intellectual property issues. Ensure you have the rights to any models or designs you incorporate into your creations.

3D-printable object designs offer a compelling way to generate income through digital products. By focusing on creating high-quality, printable designs, catering to a specific audience, and utilizing effective marketing strategies, you can establish a successful business in this growing market. Remember, understanding the technical aspects of 3D printing and keeping your designs optimized for printability are crucial for user satisfaction and repeat business.

40. High-quality, realistic 360° video tours

The world of digital products is constantly evolving, and immersive experiences are becoming increasingly popular. High-quality, realistic 360° video tours offer a unique opportunity to create engaging digital products that can generate income across various sectors. Here's a breakdown of the potential applications and revenue streams:

Target Audience and Applications:

Real Estate: Create stunning 360° video tours of properties for real estate agents, brokers, and homeowners. This allows potential buyers to virtually explore properties remotely, increasing engagement and potentially leading to faster sales or higher rental rates.

Travel and Tourism: Immerse viewers in breathtaking destinations with 360° tours of landmarks, museums, resorts, or adventure activities. These tours can be sold directly to travelers or licensed to tourism agencies to enhance their online marketing efforts.

Education and Training: Develop virtual tours of historical sites, scientific facilities, or training environments. Educational institutions and training companies can utilize these tours to enhance learning experiences and overcome geographical limitations.

Event Planning and Retail: Offer 360° tours of event venues, restaurants, or retail stores. This allows potential customers to explore the space virtually, visualize the atmosphere, and plan their visit, potentially increasing bookings and sales.

Monetization Strategies:

Direct Sales: Sell individual 360° video tours directly to your target audience. You can create a website or online store to showcase your tours and offer various pricing options.

Subscription Model: Develop a subscription service offering access to a library of your 360° video tours. This might cater to real estate agents who need access to multiple property tours or education platforms looking for a variety of virtual learning experiences.

Licensing and Partnerships: License your 360° video tours to real estate agencies, tourism boards, event venues, or travel websites. This allows them to integrate the tours into their marketing materials and potentially reach a wider audience.

Content Creation Services: Offer your expertise as a 360° video tour creator. Businesses and organizations can hire you to create customized tours of their properties, facilities, or events.

Benefits and Considerations:

Enhanced User Experience: 360° video tours provide a more realistic and interactive experience compared to traditional photos or videos. This can significantly increase user engagement and create a lasting impression.

Increased Sales and Bookings: Immersive virtual tours can help potential buyers, travelers, or clients make better-informed decisions, leading to higher conversion rates and potentially increased revenue for your clients.

Scalability and Efficiency: Once you develop the skills and equipment for creating 360° video tours, you can replicate the process for different locations, creating a scalable digital product business.

Technical Expertise: While the technology for 360° video capture is becoming more accessible, understanding camera equipment, editing software, and post-production techniques is crucial for creating high-quality, realistic tours.

Additional Tips:

Invest in Quality Equipment: High-resolution cameras and specialized rigs are essential for capturing high-quality 360° video footage.

Interactive Features: Consider incorporating interactive elements like hotspots with additional information or clickable links for a more engaging user experience.

Mobile Compatibility: Ensure your 360° video tours are optimized for viewing on mobile devices, as a large portion of online browsing happens on smartphones and tablets.

Marketing and Branding: Build a strong online presence showcasing your work and the benefits of 360° video tours. Target your marketing efforts towards businesses and organizations that can benefit from your services.

The Takeaway:

High-quality, realistic 360° video tours offer a compelling opportunity for generating income from digital products. By focusing on creating immersive user experiences, catering to specific markets, and utilizing effective marketing strategies, you can establish a successful business in this growing field. Remember, investing in good equipment and continually honing your technical skills are crucial for standing out in this competitive market.

41. Custom Architectural Renderings

Custom architectural renderings are a powerful visual tool used by architects and developers to showcase their designs. By offering these renderings as a digital product, you can cater to this specific audience and generate income through your creative skills. Here's how:

Target Audience and Applications:

Architects and Design Firms: Architects and design firms require high-quality renderings to present their proposals to clients, secure funding, and market their projects.

Real Estate Developers: Developers use architectural renderings to attract potential investors, pre-sell properties, and generate excitement for upcoming developments.

Marketing and Communication: Renderings can be used for marketing materials like brochures, websites, and social media campaigns to visually communicate the design intent and generate interest in a project.

Monetization Strategies:

Per-Project Pricing: Charge a fixed fee per project based on the complexity of the design, the number of renderings required, and the level of detail needed.

Package Deals: Offer tiered packages with varying numbers of renderings at a discounted price compared to per-project pricing. This can cater to clients with different budget needs.

Hourly Rates: Charge an hourly rate for your time spent creating the renderings. This can be suitable for smaller projects or clients with ongoing rendering needs.

Retainer Agreements: Consider offering retainer agreements to high-volume clients who require regular renderings. This can provide them with consistent service and offer you a steady stream of income.

Benefits and Considerations:

High-Value Product: Custom architectural renderings are a valuable asset for architects and developers, justifying a premium price point compared to more generic digital products.

Recurring Revenue Potential: Repeat business from satisfied clients or retainer agreements can lead to a stable income stream.

Portfolio Building: Each rendering you create adds to your portfolio, showcasing your skills and attracting new clients.

Software Expertise: Creating high-quality architectural renderings requires mastery of specialized 3D modeling and rendering software.

Additional Tips:

Understanding Architecture: Having a basic understanding of architectural principles and design concepts will allow you to create renderings that accurately represent the design intent.

Communication and Collaboration: Effective communication with your clients is crucial. Clearly understand their vision, desired level of detail, and project deadlines to ensure satisfaction.

Fast Turnaround Times: Architects and developers often operate on tight schedules. Meeting deadlines and delivering quality renderings within a defined timeframe is key to building trust and securing repeat business.

Marketing and Portfolio Development: Build a strong online presence showcasing your architectural rendering expertise. Create a portfolio website or utilize social media platforms like LinkedIn or Behance to attract potential clients.

The Takeaway:

Custom architectural renderings offer a lucrative opportunity to generate income from digital products within the architectural and design industry. By honing your skills in 3D modeling and rendering software, understanding architectural principles, and effectively communicating with clients, you can establish yourself as a valuable resource and build a successful digital product business. Remember, investing in the right software and continually refining your craft are crucial for attracting clients and creating high-value architectural renderings.

42. Original Sound Design Libraries

The power of sound is undeniable. Compelling sound effects and music can elevate any digital product, from video games and films to apps and presentations. Original sound design libraries offer a unique opportunity to generate income by providing creators with the sonic tools they need.

Target Audience and Applications:

Video Game Developers: Game developers require a vast array of sound effects to create immersive and engaging gaming experiences. Your library could offer everything from weapon sounds and character footsteps to environmental effects and user interface (UI) cues.

Film and Video Editors: Filmmakers and video editors use sound effects to enhance their productions, add realism, and evoke emotions in viewers. Your library could encompass a wide range of sound effects, from natural sounds and foley effects to cinematic transitions and sound design elements.

App Developers: App developers can utilize sound effects to improve user experience and create intuitive interfaces. Your library could provide UI sounds, notification alerts, and sound effects relevant to the specific app genre.

Content Creators: YouTubers, podcasters, and other content creators use sound effects to add polish and professionalism to their content. Your library could offer a variety of sound effects catering to different content creation needs.

Monetization Strategies:

Direct Sales: Sell individual sound effects or entire libraries directly through your own website or online marketplaces like AudioJungle or Pond5.

Subscription Model: Offer a subscription service providing access to your entire library of sound effects with regular updates and new additions.

Tiered Pricing: Create different pricing tiers based on the size and complexity of your sound libraries. Higher tiers could offer exclusive sound effects, multi-user licenses, or extended commercial use rights.

Custom Sound Design Services: In addition to pre-made libraries, offer custom sound design services for clients with specific needs. This can involve creating unique sound effects or soundtracks tailored to their projects.

Benefits and Considerations:

Recurring Revenue Potential: Subscription models and tiered pricing can generate recurring income, creating a more stable revenue stream.

Passive Income: Once your sound libraries are created, they can be sold repeatedly, generating passive income with minimal ongoing effort.

Global Market: Your digital product can be sold to a global audience of creators, maximizing your reach and income potential.

Sound Design Expertise: Creating high-quality, original sound effects requires a good understanding of sound design principles, audio editing software, and the specific needs of different content creators.

Additional Tips:

High-Quality Audio: Professional-sounding audio is crucial for creators. Invest in quality recording equipment and ensure your sound effects are clean, crisp, and well-edited.

Variety and Specificity: Offer a diverse range of sound effects catering to different genres and project types. Consider creating niche libraries focused on specific needs, such as sci-fi sound effects or historical soundscapes.

Metadata and Searchability: Use clear and descriptive metadata to tag your sound effects, allowing creators to easily find the sounds they need within your library.

Licensing and Usage Rights: Clearly define the licensing terms and usage rights associated with your sound effects. This protects your intellectual property and ensures creators understand how they can use your sounds.

The Takeaway:

Original sound design libraries offer a compelling way to generate income from digital products. By focusing on creating high-quality, diverse sound effects, catering to specific creator needs, and utilizing effective marketing strategies, you can establish a successful business in the ever-evolving world of sound design. Remember, investing in good audio equipment, mastering sound design techniques, and ensuring clear licensing terms are all essential for attracting creators and building a sustainable sonic empire!

43. Internet of Things (IoT) Applications

The Internet of Things (IoT) revolution is upon us, and it presents a wealth of opportunities to generate income through innovative digital products. By leveraging the power of connected devices and the data they generate, you can develop digital products that cater to a wide range of industries and user needs. Here's a breakdown of some promising IoT applications and how they can translate into income streams:

Target Audience and Applications:

Smart Homes: Develop digital products that control and manage smart home devices. This could include apps for lighting control, thermostat adjustment, security monitoring, or even personalized automation routines. Target these products towards homeowners seeking convenience, energy efficiency, and enhanced security.

Connected Health: Create digital products that monitor health metrics and promote wellness. This could involve wearable health trackers with data analysis dashboards, smart scales with personalized nutrition recommendations, or medication adherence applications. Cater these products to individuals seeking to manage chronic conditions, improve fitness, or simply gain insights into their health data.

Predictive Maintenance: Develop digital products for industrial IoT applications. These could involve sensor-based solutions for monitoring equipment performance, predicting maintenance needs, and preventing downtime. Target these products towards manufacturing facilities, transportation companies, and any industry that relies on heavy machinery or infrastructure.

Smart Cities: Contribute to the development of smart city initiatives with digital products for traffic management, waste collection optimization, or environmental monitoring. These products can be offered to municipalities and urban planning authorities seeking to improve efficiency and sustainability in their cities.

Monetization Strategies:

Subscription Model: Offer tiered subscription plans for access to your digital products. Basic plans could provide core functionalities, while premium tiers offer advanced features, data analysis tools, or integration with additional devices.

Freemium Model: Provide a free basic version of your digital product with limited features. This can entice users and showcase the value proposition. Premium features, data storage, or advanced functionalities can be unlocked through paid subscriptions.

Data Analytics and Insights: Develop digital products that collect and analyze data from connected devices. Offer actionable insights and reports to users, or partner with businesses willing to pay for anonymized data sets to gain valuable consumer behavior or operational efficiency insights.

Hardware Integration: If your digital product connects to specific hardware devices, consider partnering with manufacturers to pre-install your software or offer bundled packages. This can increase user adoption and generate revenue through licensing agreements.

Benefits and Considerations:

Recurring Revenue: Subscription models and data analytics services can provide a steady stream of recurring income.

Scalability: Digital products can be easily scaled to accommodate a growing user base.

Data Security and Privacy: As your product deals with user data, prioritize robust security measures and ensure transparent data collection and usage practices to build user trust.

Technical Expertise: Developing and maintaining IoT-based digital products often requires expertise in areas like sensor technology, data analytics, and secure cloud infrastructure.

Additional Tips:

Focus on User Experience: Design user-friendly interfaces for your digital products and ensure seamless interaction with connected devices.

Interoperability: Strive for compatibility with a wide range of IoT devices and platforms to maximize your user base.

Partnerships and Collaborations: Partner with hardware manufacturers, software developers, or data analytics companies to enhance your product offerings and reach a wider audience.

Innovation and Adaptability: The IoT landscape is constantly evolving. Stay updated on the latest trends and adapt your digital products to meet the ever-changing needs of the market.

The Takeaway:

The Internet of Things offers a fertile ground for generating income through innovative digital products. By focusing on specific niches, developing user-centric solutions, and prioritizing security and scalability, you can establish a successful business in this dynamic and rapidly growing market. Remember, understanding the technical complexities of IoT technology, partnering with the right players, and constantly innovating are crucial for turning the symphony of connected devices into a symphony of digital product revenue.

44. Artificial Intelligence (AI) Chatbots

AI-powered chatbots are transforming customer interactions across industries. By developing these virtual assistants as digital products, you can tap into a lucrative market offering a variety of income streams. Here's how:

Target Audience and Applications:

Customer Service: Develop chatbots for websites and mobile apps to answer customer questions, troubleshoot issues, and provide basic support. This can free up human agents for more complex inquiries while offering 24/7 customer service for businesses.

Sales and Lead Generation: Create chatbots that qualify leads, answer product inquiries, and schedule appointments. This can automate sales processes, increase lead conversion rates, and improve the overall customer experience.

Marketing and Engagement: Design chatbots for engaging marketing campaigns, providing product recommendations, or collecting user data. This allows for personalized interactions, enhances brand awareness, and drives customer engagement.

Internal Tools: Develop chatbots for employee onboarding, answering HR-related questions, or automating internal processes. This improves efficiency, reduces administrative workload, and empowers employees with self-service tools.

Monetization Strategies:

Subscription Model: Offer tiered subscription plans based on chatbot features, number of concurrent users, or the volume of inquiries handled.

Development and Deployment Fees: Charge a one-time fee for developing and deploying a custom chatbot tailored to a client's specific needs.

Per-Conversation Fee: Implement a pay-per-use model where clients are charged based on the number of user interactions with the chatbot.

Training and Support Services: Provide ongoing training and support services for clients using your chatbot platform, ensuring optimal performance and user experience.

Benefits and Considerations:

Improved Customer Experience: Chatbots offer 24/7 availability, answer common questions quickly, and personalize interactions, leading to higher customer satisfaction.

Cost Savings: Chatbots can automate repetitive tasks, reduce the need for human customer service agents, and improve operational efficiency for businesses.

Data Collection and Insights: Chatbots can collect valuable customer data and usage patterns, providing businesses with insights to improve products, personalize marketing campaigns, and optimize user experience.

Technical Expertise: Developing effective chatbots requires expertise in natural language processing (NLP), machine learning, and chatbot development platforms.

Additional Tips:

Focus on Natural Language Understanding: Ensure your chatbot can understand natural language queries and respond in a way that is clear, informative, and engaging.

Personalization: Integrate user data to personalize chatbot interactions, offer relevant recommendations, and improve customer satisfaction.

Omnichannel Integration: Allow your chatbot to seamlessly integrate with different communication channels like websites, messaging apps, and social media platforms.

Data Security and Transparency: Prioritize data security and be transparent about how user data is collected, stored, and used.

The Takeaway:

AI chatbots represent a powerful tool for businesses to improve customer interactions, automate tasks, and generate valuable data. By focusing on user experience, natural language processing, and data security, you can develop compelling AI chatbot solutions as digital products. Utilize a combination of monetization strategies to cater to various business needs and establish a successful revenue stream in the ever-evolving world of AI-powered customer service. Remember, investing in the right NLP tools and chatbot development platforms is crucial for creating intelligent and engaging virtual assistants.

45. Custom Enterprise Software

In today's competitive business landscape, many companies require software solutions that cater to their unique needs and workflows. Custom enterprise software, developed specifically for a client's operations, offers a lucrative opportunity to generate income through digital products.

Target Audience and Applications:

Large Enterprises: Large organizations often have complex business processes that can't be addressed by off-the-shelf software. Develop custom solutions for areas like inventory management, customer relationship management (CRM), or enterprise resource planning (ERP).

Specialized Industries: Certain industries have specific needs not met by generic software. Create custom solutions for healthcare data management, legal document management, or project management in engineering firms.

Internal Processes: Develop software to automate internal tasks within a company, such as HR onboarding processes, expense management systems, or data analysis dashboards for specific departments.

Monetization Strategies:

Project-Based Pricing: Charge a fixed fee based on the scope and complexity of the software development project. This is a common approach for one-time custom builds.

Time and Materials Billing: Bill clients based on the time spent by your development team and the resources used to create the software. This is suitable for projects with evolving requirements.

Subscription Model with Ongoing Support: Develop the software with a subscription model in mind. Clients pay a recurring fee for access to the software and ongoing maintenance and support services.

Licensing and Revenue Sharing: In some cases, you might consider licensing your custom software to other companies with similar needs. This can generate additional revenue streams beyond the initial development project.

Benefits and Considerations:

High-Value Product: Custom enterprise software offers significant value to businesses by streamlining operations, improving efficiency, and providing a competitive advantage. This justifies a premium price point compared to generic software.

Recurring Revenue Potential: Subscription models and ongoing support contracts can provide a steady stream of income.

Long-Term Client Relationships: Developing custom software often leads to long-term client relationships as you provide ongoing support and potential future software enhancements.

Development Team Expertise: Building custom enterprise software requires a skilled development team with expertise in various programming languages, software development methodologies, and understanding of specific industry needs.

Additional Tips:

Clear Project Scoping and Requirements Gathering: Thoroughly understand your client's needs and ensure clear project scope definition before development begins. This minimizes the risk of scope creep and project delays.

Agile Development Methodology: Consider using agile development methodologies to deliver software in increments and gather continuous client feedback. This ensures the final product aligns with the client's evolving needs.

Data Security and Scalability: Prioritize data security measures as you deal with potentially sensitive business information. Ensure the software can scale to accommodate future growth within the client's organization.

Maintenance and Support: Provide ongoing maintenance and support services to ensure the software continues to function optimally and address any bugs or emerging issues.

The Takeaway:

Custom enterprise software offers a compelling way to generate income through digital products, catering to unique business needs. By focusing on building strong client relationships, understanding industry specifics, and employing effective development practices, you can establish a successful business in this high-value market. Remember, assembling a skilled development team and ensuring clear communication throughout the project lifecycle are crucial for delivering successful custom software solutions.

46. Industry-Specific Data Analysis Tools

The power of data analytics is undeniable across all industries. By developing industry-specific data analysis tools as digital products, you can cater to the unique needs of different sectors and generate income through valuable insights.

Target Audience and Applications:

Finance and Banking: Develop tools for analyzing financial data, identifying fraud risks, optimizing investment strategies, or predicting market trends. Target these tools towards banks, wealth management firms, and financial institutions.

Retail and E-commerce: Create data analysis tools for understanding customer behavior, optimizing product placement, managing inventory levels, and personalizing marketing campaigns. Target these tools towards retailers, online marketplaces, and e-commerce businesses.

Healthcare and Pharmaceuticals: Develop tools for analyzing patient data, tracking disease outbreaks, conducting clinical trials, and optimizing drug development processes. Target these tools towards hospitals, research institutions, and pharmaceutical companies.

Manufacturing and Supply Chain: Create data analysis tools for monitoring production lines, predicting equipment failures, optimizing supply chain logistics, and improving product quality control. Target these tools towards manufacturers, logistics companies, and industrial facilities.

Monetization Strategies:

Subscription Model: Offer tiered subscription plans based on the features, data storage capacity, and user access levels of your data analysis tool.

Freemium Model: Provide a basic version of your tool with limited features for free. This allows users to experience the tool's value and incentivizes them to upgrade to a premium subscription plan for advanced functionalities.

Pay-Per-Use Model: Implement a system where users pay based on the amount of data they analyze or the specific features they use within your tool.

Customization and Integration Services: In addition to the core data analysis tool, offer customization services to tailor it to specific industry needs or integrate it with existing data infrastructure.

Benefits and Considerations:

High-Value Niche Products: Industry-specific data analysis tools cater to a focused audience and solve specific pain points, justifying a premium price point compared to generic data analysis platforms.

Recurring Revenue Potential: Subscription models and pay-per-use structures can create a steady stream of recurring income.

Domain Expertise: Developing effective industry-specific data analysis tools requires a deep understanding of the data sets, challenges, and analytical needs of the target audience.

Data Security and Compliance: Prioritize data security measures and ensure your tools comply with industry regulations regarding data privacy and security.

Additional Tips:

Focus on User-Friendly Interface and Visualization: Ensure your data analysis tool offers a user-friendly interface with clear visualizations and actionable insights, even for users with limited technical expertise.

Industry-Specific Features: Integrate functionalities and data analysis methods relevant to the specific industry. For example, a healthcare tool might offer features for patient cohort analysis, while a retail tool might focus on customer segmentation and purchase behavior analysis.

Partnerships and Integrations: Partner with industry leaders or data providers to access specialized datasets and enhance the value proposition of your tools.

Stay Updated on Industry Trends: The data analytics landscape is constantly evolving. Keep up-to-date with emerging technologies and industry trends to ensure your tools remain relevant and valuable.

The Takeaway:

Industry-specific data analysis tools offer a lucrative opportunity to generate income through digital products. By focusing on understanding industry needs, developing user-friendly interfaces, and prioritizing data security, you can establish a successful business in this niche market. Remember, combining domain expertise with data analysis best practices is crucial for creating valuable tools that empower businesses to unlock the full potential of their data.

47. Immersive Learning Experiences

Immersive learning experiences, powered by virtual reality (VR) and augmented reality (AR), are revolutionizing education. By developing these captivating digital products, you can tap into a growing market seeking innovative ways to learn and generate income.

Target Audience and Applications:

K-12 Education: Create VR field trips that transport students to historical landmarks, the depths of the ocean, or even the surface of Mars. Develop AR applications that overlay interactive elements onto textbooks or classroom environments, bringing complex concepts to life.

Higher Education: Design VR simulations for medical students to practice procedures, engineering students to test virtual prototypes, or language learners to immerse themselves in foreign cultures.

Corporate Training: Develop AR training modules for employees to learn new skills in a safe and controlled environment, such as practicing safety protocols or conducting product demonstrations.

Monetization Strategies:

Subscription Model: Offer tiered subscription plans for schools or training institutions based on the number of users, content access, and features like downloadable VR experiences.

Freemium Model: Provide a basic version of your VR experience or AR app for free, showcasing its potential. Charge for premium content, advanced features, or access to a library of immersive learning modules.

Individual User Licensing: For certain VR experiences, consider individual user licenses for students or trainees, allowing them to access the content on their own devices.

Content Partnerships: Develop partnerships with educational institutions, museums, or historical sites to create exclusive VR field trips or AR content based on their expertise and resources.

Benefits and Considerations:

Enhanced Learning Outcomes: Immersive learning experiences can improve knowledge retention, boost engagement, and cater to diverse learning styles compared to traditional methods.

Scalability and Accessibility: Digital products can be easily scaled to reach a wider audience across geographical boundaries.

Content Development Expertise: Creating compelling VR and AR experiences requires expertise in 3D modeling, game development, educational content creation, and understanding of the target audience's learning needs.

Hardware Compatibility: Ensure your VR experiences are compatible with available VR headsets and your AR apps function seamlessly on various mobile devices.

Additional Tips:

Focus on User Experience and Interactivity: Make your VR experiences and AR apps engaging and interactive, allowing users to explore, experiment, and actively participate in the learning process.

Data-Driven Learning Analytics: Integrate data analytics features to track user behavior and learning progress within your VR/AR experiences. This can be valuable for educators and trainers, and can inform future content development.

Accessibility Features: Ensure your immersive learning experiences are accessible to users with disabilities, including options for different learning styles and physical limitations.

Embrace New Technologies: The VR and AR landscape is constantly evolving. Stay updated on emerging technologies like haptic feedback suits or AR glasses to enhance the learning experience further.

The Takeaway:

Immersive learning experiences powered by VR and AR offer a unique opportunity to generate income through digital products. By focusing on creating engaging content, prioritizing accessibility, and staying updated on technological advancements, you can establish a successful business in this exciting and rapidly growing market. Remember, investing in the right development tools and partnering with educational institutions can be instrumental in creating impactful and in-demand immersive learning experiences.

48. Personalized Learning Management Systems (LMS) with Advanced Reporting

In the digital product landscape, where knowledge is a key currency, Personalized Learning Management Systems (PLMS) with advanced reporting are emerging as powerful tools to maximize income. Here's how:

Personalized Learning Paths:

Targeted Content Delivery: PLMS can identify a user's strengths and weaknesses, recommending specific courses or modules that address their individual needs. This targeted approach keeps users engaged and actively purchasing new content relevant to their goals.

Adaptive Learning: Advanced PLMS can adjust the difficulty and pace of learning based on user performance. This ensures users are constantly challenged, preventing disengagement and encouraging them to seek out more advanced (and potentially more expensive) content.

Advanced Reporting for Revenue Insights:

User Engagement Analytics: PLMS with granular reporting can track user behavior, identifying popular content, completion rates, and areas where users struggle. This data allows creators to tailor future content offerings to maximize user engagement and potential purchases.

Sales & Conversion Tracking: Advanced reporting can track user journeys, identifying which learning paths or content bundles lead to higher conversion rates for premium features or additional courses. This allows creators to optimize pricing strategies and product recommendations.

Learning ROI Measurement: PLMS reports can demonstrate the value proposition of digital learning products. By tracking user progress and knowledge gain, creators can showcase the impact of their content on user skills and justify premium pricing.

Additional Revenue Streams:

Subscription Models: PLMS can facilitate subscription-based access to content libraries, with tiered plans offering various levels of depth and features. Advanced reporting helps creators identify optimal subscription pricing and content packages.

Microtransactions: PLMS can enable microtransactions for specific learning modules or assessments, allowing users to customize their learning experience and creators to earn revenue from smaller content pieces.

Overall, PLMS with advanced reporting offer a comprehensive solution for digital product creators by:
• Personalizing the learning experience, boosting user engagement.
• Providing valuable data for content optimization and pricing strategies.
• Enabling new revenue streams through subscriptions and microtransactions.

By leveraging the power of personalization and data-driven insights, PLMS can empower creators to maximize income from their digital learning products.

49. Custom E-commerce Stores with Advanced Personalization Features

In the thriving world of digital products, custom e-commerce stores with advanced personalization features are becoming game-changers for creators looking to maximize their income. Here's how these stores can unlock significant revenue potential:

Hyper-Targeted Product Recommendations:

AI-powered Recommendations: Leveraging customer data like browsing history, purchase behavior, and demographics, these stores can recommend relevant digital products to each visitor. This increases the likelihood of impulse purchases and conversions.

Dynamic Product Bundles: AI can curate personalized product bundles based on user needs and interests. Imagine suggesting a design software package with specific fonts and tutorials based on a user's downloaded assets.

Contextual Upselling and Cross-selling: Highlight relevant upgrades, add-ons, or complementary digital products based on the user's current selection. Imagine suggesting advanced photography filters when a user purchases a photo editing software.

Personalized User Experience:

Curated Product Displays: Showcase different digital products based on user preferences. A musician browsing for music production software might see different options than a video editor.

Dynamic Pricing and Promotions: Offer personalized discounts or tiered pricing based on user history or loyalty programs. This incentivizes purchases and fosters long-term customer relationships.

Interactive Product Demos: Integrate personalized product demos tailored to user needs. Imagine showcasing specific features of a language learning app based on the user's chosen language.

Enhanced Customer Engagement:

Personalized Content Marketing: Deliver targeted blog posts, tutorials, or webinars based on user interests. This keeps customers engaged and reinforces the value proposition of your digital products.

Interactive Product Reviews: Encourage personalized product reviews by prompting users to share their specific experiences with different features. This builds trust and social proof, influencing other potential buyers.

Loyalty Programs and Gamification: Implement loyalty programs that reward repeat purchases and incentivize exploring new digital products within your store. Gamification elements like badges or challenges can further boost customer engagement.

Measurable Revenue Growth:

A/B Testing and Optimization: Personalization features allow for constant A/B testing of different recommendation algorithms, product displays, and pricing strategies. This data-driven approach helps optimize the store for maximum conversions.

Customer Lifetime Value (CLTV) Focus: Personalized experiences foster customer loyalty, leading to repeat purchases and a higher CLTV.

Overall, custom e-commerce stores with advanced personalization features offer a powerful platform for digital product creators by:
• Creating a frictionless buying journey with hyper-targeted recommendations.
• Building deeper customer relationships through personalized experiences.
• Increasing conversions and revenue through data-driven optimization.

By investing in a personalized e-commerce store, digital product creators can unlock significant revenue potential and build a loyal customer base in the ever-evolving digital marketplace.

50. Digital Twins of Physical Products or Systems

Digital twins are revolutionizing how companies design, operate, and maintain physical products and systems. But beyond core functionalities, digital twins offer a unique opportunity to generate income through digital products and services. This note explores how digital twins can be leveraged as a revenue stream.

What are Digital Twins?

A digital twin is a virtual representation of a physical product or system. It combines data from sensors attached to the physical counterpart with software models to create a real-time reflection of its performance, behavior, and condition. This digital replica can be used for various purposes, including:

Predictive maintenance: By analyzing sensor data, digital twins can predict potential failures before they occur, allowing for proactive maintenance and reducing downtime.

Remote monitoring and diagnostics: Engineers can monitor the health and performance of physical assets remotely through the digital twin, enabling faster troubleshooting and issue resolution.

Product optimization: Digital twins can be used to simulate different scenarios and test design changes in a virtual environment, leading to improved product performance and efficiency.

Monetization through Digital Twins

Here's how companies can leverage digital twins to generate income:

Subscription-based services: Companies can offer access to the digital twin platform and data insights through monthly or annual subscriptions. This could be targeted towards maintenance teams, operators, or even end-users.

Predictive maintenance as a service (PdMaaS): Leveraging the predictive capabilities of the digital twin, companies can offer PdMaaS contracts, where they take responsibility for maintenance based on real-time data analysis and alerts.

Data-driven insights and analytics: The vast amount of data collected by the digital twin can be analyzed to generate valuable insights for customers. This data can be packaged into reports or dashboards, providing actionable intelligence to improve operations, optimize resource allocation, and identify new revenue opportunities.

Virtual training and simulation: Digital twins can be used to create realistic training simulations for technicians and operators. This can be offered as a standalone service or bundled with the digital twin platform.

Performance optimization services: By analyzing the digital twin data, companies can offer consulting services to help customers optimize the performance of their physical assets.

Benefits of Digital Twin Revenue Streams

Recurring revenue: Subscription-based services and PdMaaS contracts provide a predictable and recurring revenue stream.

Customer lifetime value: Digital twin services create a sticky relationship with customers, as they become reliant on the data and insights provided.

Differentiation: Offering digital twin solutions can differentiate a company from competitors and create a new value proposition.

Challenges and Considerations

Initial investment: Developing and implementing a digital twin platform requires a significant upfront investment in technology and expertise.

Data security: The vast amount of data collected by the digital twin needs robust security measures to protect against cyberattacks.

Customer adoption: Educating customers about the value proposition of digital twins is crucial for successful adoption.

Conclusion
Digital twins hold immense potential for generating revenue through innovative digital products and services. By leveraging the data and insights from these virtual representations, companies can create new business models, strengthen customer relationships, and gain a competitive edge in the digital age.

51. Ebooks on Common Interests

Ebooks have become a popular digital product, offering readers convenient and affordable access to information. But with a saturated market, standing out requires a strategic approach. Here, we explore the potential of ebooks on common interests as a source of income.

The Power of Common Interests

People are drawn to content that resonates with their passions and hobbies. Common interests cover a broad spectrum, from cooking and gardening to music production and woodworking. By focusing on specific niches within these interests, you can tap into a dedicated audience eager for in-depth information and practical guidance.

Benefits of Ebooks on Common Interests

Targeted Audience: A niche focus allows you to tailor your content to the specific needs and desires of a well-defined audience.

Passionate Readers: People with strong interests are more likely to actively seek out and pay for high-quality information.

Repeat Business: By establishing yourself as an expert in a niche, you can build a loyal following that will purchase future ebooks related to that interest.

Lower Competition: While general topics may be crowded, niche markets often have less competition, making it easier to get your ebook noticed.

Developing Profitable Ebooks

Identify Your Niche: Research popular interests and find a specific sub-category where you possess expertise or a unique perspective.

Solve Problems, Offer Value: Focus on providing practical solutions to common challenges faced by your target audience.

High-Quality Content: Invest in well-written, informative content with clear instructions, engaging visuals, and actionable advice.

Targeted Marketing: Promote your ebook through social media groups, online communities, and influencer partnerships relevant to your niche.

Monetization Strategies

Direct Sales: Sell your ebook directly through your website or online marketplaces like Amazon Kindle Direct Publishing.

Subscription Model: Offer exclusive ebooks or bonus content as part of a monthly subscription service.

Bundled Products: Combine your ebook with additional resources like video tutorials or cheat sheets for a higher price point.

Additional Considerations

Competition Research: Analyze successful ebooks in your niche to understand reader preferences and content gaps.

Pricing Strategy: Balance value proposition with market expectations and ensure your ebook offers a fair return on investment for readers.

Self-Publishing vs. Traditional Publishing: Consider whether self-publishing affords you greater control or if partnering with a publisher provides wider reach.

Ebooks on common interests offer a lucrative opportunity in the digital product space. By focusing on a well-defined niche, providing valuable content, and employing effective marketing strategies, you can build a loyal audience and generate income through your expertise and passion.

52. Printable Planners & Templates

The desire for organization and productivity has fueled the rise of printable planners and templates. This digital product category offers a unique opportunity for creativity and income generation. Here's a deep dive into how to leverage this thriving niche.

The Allure of Printables

Printable planners and templates cater to a vast audience seeking structure and personalization. From budget trackers and meal planners to habit trackers and project management templates, these digital downloads offer a customizable and cost-effective solution for individuals and businesses alike.

Advantages of Printables

Broad Appeal: The wide range of planner and template applications caters to diverse needs, ensuring a large potential market.

Customization: Users can personalize templates to fit their specific workflows and preferences, increasing value perception.

Scalability: Once created, the digital product can be sold countless times, generating recurring income.

Low Barriers to Entry: Minimal upfront investment is required compared to physical products, making it accessible for new entrepreneurs.

Creating Profitable Printables

Identify Your Niche: Within the vast realm of printables, focus on a specific area like student planners, business productivity templates, or health and fitness trackers.

Focus on User Experience: Design visually appealing, user-friendly templates with clear instructions and intuitive layouts.

Value Proposition: Go beyond basic layouts. Offer valuable features like trackers, checklists, goal-setting sections, and inspirational quotes.

Multiple Formats: Provide printables in various sizes (A4, Letter) and file formats (PDF, JPG) for user convenience.

Monetization Strategies

Direct Sales: Sell individual printables or collections through your website or online marketplaces like Etsy.

Subscription Model: Offer access to a library of downloadable printables for a monthly or annual fee.

Bundles: Combine different planner themes or templates into attractive bundles at a discounted price.

Freemium Model: Offer a basic version for free and premium versions with additional features or layouts for purchase.

Additional Considerations

Market Research: Analyze trending themes and identify unmet needs within your chosen niche.

Marketing and Promotion: Promote your printables on social media, relevant online communities, and through collaborations with productivity bloggers.

Product Differentiation: Stand out by offering unique features, high-quality design, or niche-specific themes.

Printable planners and templates offer a dynamic and lucrative niche in the digital product world. By identifying a target audience, creating valuable printables, and implementing strategic marketing, you can establish a thriving business built on organization and user empowerment.

53. Stock Photos for Specific Niches

Stock photography is a well-established digital product market. However, with millions of images available, competition is fierce. Here's how to leverage niche stock photos as a source of income and carve out your space in this booming industry.

The Power of Niche

General stock photo websites often overflow with generic images. By focusing on specific niches, you can cater to a targeted audience with unique visual needs. This approach offers several advantages:

Reduced Competition: Niche markets have fewer photographers, giving your photos a higher chance of being seen and purchased.

Premium Pricing: Highly specific photos command a premium price due to their limited availability.

Loyal Customers: Building a reputation within a niche fosters repeat business from satisfied customers within that community.

Identifying Profitable Niches

Passion Meets Demand: Consider your photographic expertise and identify niches where your skills align with specific visual needs (e.g., organic farming, woodworking, sustainable living).

Emerging Trends: Research trending topics and hobbies that lack readily available stock photos.

Untapped Industries: Look for niche industries with a growing online presence that might not be well-served by existing stock photo platforms.

Creating High-Value Niche Photos

Authenticity and Storytelling: Go beyond generic shots. Capture the essence of your niche with genuine emotions, real-life scenarios, and diverse representation.

Technical Expertise: Master lighting, composition, and editing techniques to create visually appealing and high-quality photos.

Keyword Optimization: Use relevant keywords in your photo titles and descriptions to ensure your images are discoverable by niche buyers.

Monetization Strategies

Microstock Platforms: Sell your photos through established microstock platforms like Shutterstock or Adobe Stock, catering to a wider audience within your niche.

Niche Marketplaces: Explore niche-specific stock photo platforms that cater to specific industries or interests.

Direct Licensing: Offer direct licensing deals to businesses or content creators within your niche for exclusive use of your photos.

Additional Considerations

Legal Requirements: Ensure you have the necessary licenses and releases for any recognizable people, property, or trademarks in your photos.

Building a Portfolio: Develop a strong portfolio showcasing the breadth and quality of your niche photography.

Community Engagement: Network with industry professionals, bloggers, and social media influencers within your niche for potential collaborations and marketing opportunities.

Niche stock photos offer a lucrative opportunity for photographers in the digital product space. By focusing on a specific audience, capturing high-quality, relevant images, and implementing strategic marketing within your niche.

54. Social Media Templates

The ever-growing demand for engaging social media content has created a lucrative market for social media templates. These digital products offer businesses and individuals a time-saving and visually appealing way to elevate their online presence. Here's a roadmap to profiting from this thriving niche.

The Rise of Social Media Templates

Creating consistent, high-quality social media content can be time-consuming and challenging. Social media templates provide a pre-designed framework that users can customize with their own text, images, and branding. This empowers them to:

Save Time & Resources: Templates eliminate the need to start from scratch, streamlining the content creation process.

Maintain Brand Consistency: Templates ensure a cohesive visual identity across all social media platforms.

Enhance Content Appeal: Professionally designed templates elevate the visual impact of social media posts.

Benefits of Selling Social Media Templates

Recurring Revenue: Offer template bundles or subscriptions for ongoing income.

Scalability: Sell the same template countless times, maximizing profits from a single creation.

Low Maintenance: Once designed, templates require minimal upkeep compared to physical products.

Broad Market Appeal: Businesses and individuals across various industries rely on social media, creating a vast potential customer base.

Developing Profitable Social Media Templates

Identify Your Niche: Focus on specific social media platforms (Instagram, Facebook Stories) or cater to a particular industry (e.g., real estate, e-commerce).

Variety & Functionality: Offer a range of templates with different layouts, colors, and functionalities (quotes, testimonials, product promotions).

Ease of Use: Templates should be user-friendly and easily customizable within popular design platforms like Canva or Photoshop.

Mobile Optimization: Ensure templates adapt well to mobile viewing formats, considering the dominance of mobile social media use.

Monetization Strategies

Direct Sales: Sell individual templates or collections through your website or online marketplaces like Etsy or Creative Market.

Subscription Model: Offer access to a library of downloadable templates for a monthly or annual fee.

Freemium Model: Provide basic templates for free with premium options offering more features and design variations.

Software Integrations: Develop templates compatible with specific social media management platforms and offer them within those platforms.

Additional Considerations

Market Research: Analyze trending social media content formats and identify gaps in available templates.

Stay Updated: Keep your templates current with evolving social media trends and platform updates.

Marketing & Promotion: Showcase your templates through social media marketing, tutorials, and collaborations with social media influencers.

Conclusion
Social media templates offer a compelling opportunity to generate income from digital products. By catering to a specific niche, designing user-friendly templates, and implementing effective marketing strategies, you can help businesses and individuals streamline their social media presence and build a thriving online business.

55. Basic Website Themes

The digital landscape thrives on user-friendly and visually appealing websites. Basic website themes offer a cost-effective and efficient solution for individuals and businesses to establish their online presence. Here's a breakdown of how this niche can be a springboard for generating income through digital products.

The Power of Simplicity

Basic website themes cater to users who need a functional and attractive website without extensive customization. They offer a pre-built framework with features like:

Responsive design: Ensures the website adapts seamlessly to different screen sizes (desktop, mobile, tablet).

Content management system (CMS) integration: Allows users to easily add, edit, and manage website content.

Essential functionalities: Includes features like contact forms, galleries, and social media integration.

Advantages of Selling Basic Website Themes

Broad Market Appeal: The demand for basic website themes is vast, encompassing businesses, freelancers, bloggers, and personal projects.

Recurring Revenue: Offer theme bundles or subscription services with access to multiple themes and updates.

Scalability: Sell the same theme countless times, maximizing profits from a single development effort.

Low Maintenance: Themes require minimal maintenance once designed and can be easily updated for compatibility with evolving platforms.

Developing Profitable Basic Website Themes

Niche Focus: While catering to a broad audience, consider offering themes tailored for specific industries (restaurants, photographers) for a competitive edge.

User Experience (UX) Focus: Prioritize clean layouts, intuitive navigation, and mobile responsiveness for optimal user experience.

Customization Options: Offer basic customization features like color palettes, font changes, and logo integration.

Clear Documentation and Support: Provide user-friendly documentation and responsive support to ensure customer satisfaction.

Monetization Strategies

Direct Sales: Sell individual themes or theme packs through your website or theme marketplaces like ThemeForest or TemplateMonster.

Freemium Model: Offer a basic theme with limited features for free and premium versions with advanced functionalities and customization options.

Subscription Model: Provide access to a library of downloadable themes and future updates for a monthly or annual subscription fee.

Extended Services: Offer optional add-on services like theme installation, customization, and ongoing maintenance for a premium price.

Additional Considerations

Market Research: Analyze popular website design trends and identify features most sought after by users.

Theme Quality & Performance: Ensure your themes are built with clean code, optimized for loading speed, and regularly tested for compatibility with various CMS platforms.

Marketing & Promotion: Showcase your themes through online demos, showcase websites built with your themes, and targeted social media advertising.

Conclusion

Basic website themes offer a lucrative opportunity for developers and designers in the digital product space. By focusing on user experience, providing customization options, and employing effective marketing strategies, you can help individuals and businesses establish their online presence and build a sustainable income from your digital products.

56. Simple Meal Plans

In today's fast-paced world, busy individuals crave convenient and healthy meal planning solutions. Simple meal plans, offered as digital products, address this growing demand, providing a lucrative opportunity for those with culinary expertise. Here's a roadmap to profiting from this flavorful niche.

The Appeal of Simple Meal Plans

People are overwhelmed with meal planning challenges: lack of time, dietary restrictions, and indecisiveness. Simple meal plans offer a time-saving and stress-free solution by providing:

Pre-defined meals: Eliminate the "what's for dinner?" dilemma with pre-planned breakfasts, lunches, dinners, and snacks.

Focus on simplicity: Easy-to-follow recipes with readily available ingredients ensure meal preparation is manageable.

Customization options: Offer basic templates with room for dietary adjustments and personal preferences.

Advantages of Selling Simple Meal Plans

Recurring Revenue: Offer monthly or weekly meal plan subscriptions for a steady income stream.

Scalability: Sell the same meal plans countless times, maximizing profits from your content creation.

Low Maintenance: Once developed, meal plans require minimal upkeep compared to physical products.

Broad Market Appeal: People across demographics and lifestyles seek convenient meal solutions, creating a vast potential customer base.

Developing Profitable Simple Meal Plans

Identify Your Niche: Focus on specific dietary needs (vegetarian, gluten-free, paleo) or cater to families, busy professionals, or budget-conscious individuals.

Variety & Balance: Offer a range of delicious and nutritious meals across different cuisines and dietary needs.

Clear Instructions & Shopping Lists: Provide detailed recipe instructions and comprehensive shopping lists for hassle-free meal preparation.

Visually Appealing Content: Include high-quality photos of finished dishes to entice potential customers.

Monetization Strategies

Direct Sales: Sell individual meal plans or subscription packages through your website or online marketplaces like Etsy.

Subscription Model: Offer tiered subscription plans with access to a library of downloadable meal plans and bonus content (grocery delivery discounts, recipe tutorials).

Freemium Model: Provide a limited sample meal plan for free and premium versions with a wider variety of options and customization features.

Additional Considerations

Market Research: Analyze trending food preferences, dietary restrictions, and meal planning challenges faced by your target audience.

Seasonal Variations: Incorporate seasonal ingredients and recipes to maintain interest and cater to changing tastes.

Marketing & Promotion: Promote your meal plans through food blogs, social media influencers, and collaborations with meal delivery services.

Building Trust & Expertise: Offer free recipe samples, cooking tutorials, and establish yourself as a reliable source of healthy and delicious meal planning solutions.

Conclusion
Simple meal plans offer a delicious opportunity to generate income from digital products. By focusing on a specific niche, creating mouthwatering and convenient meal plans, and implementing effective marketing strategies, you can help people eat well and build a thriving online business.

57. Stock Audio & Video Clips

The world of visual and audio content creation relies heavily on stock libraries. Stock audio and video clips offer creators a vast selection of royalty-free sounds and visuals to elevate their projects. Let's explore how you can leverage this dynamic niche to generate income through digital products.

The Power of Stock

Stock libraries cater to a diverse clientele, including:

Video editors: Youtubers, filmmakers, and marketing agencies use stock footage to enhance their video productions.

Content creators: Podcasters, bloggers, and social media influencers utilize stock audio for intros, outros, and background music.

Businesses: Stock videos and music add professionalism to presentations, marketing materials, and explainer videos.

Advantages of Selling Stock Audio & Video

Recurring Revenue: Each download generates income, creating a continuous revenue stream.

Passive Income: Once created, your clips can be downloaded and sold countless times.

Scalability: Build a library of diverse clips to cater to a wider range of customers.

Global Market: Digital products transcend geographical boundaries, reaching a vast audience.

Creating High-Value Stock Clips

Audio: Focus on high-quality recordings across a variety of genres (sound effects, background music, voiceovers).

Video: Capture visually appealing footage covering different themes (nature landscapes, business settings, product demonstrations).

Keyword Optimization: Use relevant keywords in titles and descriptions to ensure your clips are easily discoverable.

Variety & Relevance: Offer a diverse range of clips that address current trends and user needs.

Monetization Strategies

Microstock Platforms: Sell your clips through established platforms like Shutterstock, Adobe Stock, or Pond5, reaching a broad audience.

Niche Marketplaces: Explore niche-specific stock libraries catering to a particular industry or content type.

Direct Licensing: Offer exclusive licensing deals to businesses or creators for specific projects.

Additional Considerations

Legal Requirements: Ensure you have the proper licenses for any copyrighted music or recognizable elements in your clips.

Technical Expertise: Master audio and video editing techniques to create professional-quality stock content.

Market Research: Analyze trending video and audio styles in your chosen niche to identify content gaps.

Building a Portfolio: Develop a strong portfolio showcasing the breadth and quality of your stock library.

Conclusion
Stock audio and video clips offer a lucrative opportunity for creators and videographers in the

digital product space. By focusing on high-quality content, strategic keyword optimization, and effective marketing within your niche, you can establish a thriving business and soundtrack the success of countless creative projects.

58. Basic Lightroom Presets

Lightroom is a popular photo editing software used by photographers of all levels. Basic Lightroom presets offer a time-saving and easy-to-use way to achieve professional-looking edits. Here's a roadmap to profiting from this niche in the digital product space.

The Allure of Presets

Photographers, especially beginners, often struggle with achieving consistent and visually appealing edits. Basic Lightroom presets provide a one-click solution, transforming photos with pre-defined adjustments to color, tone, and exposure.

Advantages of Selling Basic Lightroom Presets

Recurring Revenue: Offer preset packs or subscription models for ongoing income.

Scalability: Sell the same presets countless times, maximizing profits from your creation.

Low Maintenance: Once developed, presets require minimal upkeep compared to physical products.

Broad Market Appeal: Photographers of various skill levels seek efficient editing solutions, creating a vast potential customer base.

Developing Profitable Basic Presets

Identify Your Niche: Focus on specific photography styles (portraiture, travel, landscape) or cater to beginners who need fundamental editing tools.

User-Friendly & Customizable: Presets should be easy to apply and offer basic customization options for exposure and white balance.

Cohesive Collection: Create a preset pack with a variety of styles that complement each other and achieve a consistent aesthetic.

Clear Instructions & Support: Provide user-friendly instructions for preset installation and basic editing guidance.

Monetization Strategies

Direct Sales: Sell individual preset packs or collections through your website or online marketplaces like Etsy or Creative Market.

Subscription Model: Offer access to a library of downloadable presets and future updates for a monthly or annual fee.

Freemium Model: Provide a limited sample preset for free and premium packs with a wider range of styles and advanced editing capabilities.

Additional Considerations

Market Research: Analyze trending photography styles and identify editing challenges faced by your target audience.

Before & After Examples: Showcase the transformative power of your presets with high-quality "before and after" photo comparisons.

Marketing & Promotion: Promote your presets through photography blogs, social media influencers, and targeted advertising to photographers.

Compatibility Testing: Ensure your presets are compatible with various Lightroom versions and camera formats.

Conclusion
Basic Lightroom presets offer a bright opportunity to generate income from digital products. By catering to a specific niche, creating user-friendly presets, and implementing effective marketing strategies, you can help photographers streamline their editing workflow and establish a successful business.

59. Knitting or Crochet Patterns

The world of knitting and crochet is booming, driven by a surge in interest in crafting and DIY projects. This surge creates a lucrative opportunity to sell knitting or crochet patterns as digital products. Here's a detailed guide to profiting from your crafting expertise:

The Power of Patterns

People of all skill levels seek well-designed patterns to create beautiful and functional knitted or crocheted items. Selling patterns offers several advantages:

Recurring Revenue: Each download generates income, creating a steady revenue stream.

Passive Income: Once designed, a pattern can be downloaded and sold countless times.

Global Market: Digital products transcend geographical boundaries, reaching a vast audience of crafters.

Low Maintenance: Once created, patterns require minimal upkeep compared to physical products.

Crafting Profitable Knitting & Crochet Patterns

Identify Your Niche: Focus on specific types of projects (garments, accessories, home décor) or cater to skill levels (beginner, intermediate, advanced).

Clear Instructions & Visuals: Provide detailed written instructions with step-by-step photos or diagrams for clarity.

Multiple Sizes & Variations: Offer patterns in a range of sizes (adult, child) or include variations for customization.

Technical Accuracy & Abbreviations: Ensure your patterns are free of errors, use standard abbreviations, and provide a glossary if necessary.

Monetization Strategies

Direct Sales: Sell individual patterns or pattern packs through your own website or online marketplaces like Ravelry, Etsy, or LoveCrafts.

Subscription Model: Offer exclusive patterns or bonus content as part of a monthly or annual subscription service.

Pattern Bundles: Combine different patterns into attractive bundles at a discounted price.

Additional Considerations

Market Research: Analyze trending styles and techniques in knitting and crochet to identify in-demand patterns.

High-Quality Photos: Showcase the finished product with professional-looking photos to entice potential buyers.

Community Engagement: Promote your patterns through social media groups, online forums, and collaborations with yarn stores or knitting/crochet influencers.

Copyright Protection: Include copyright information in your patterns and consider offering extended licenses for commercial use (e.g., selling finished products made with your pattern).

Beyond the Basics

Video Tutorials: Complement your written patterns with video tutorials demonstrating key techniques, especially for beginners.

Kits & Supplies: Partner with yarn stores or online retailers to offer project kits that include yarn and other materials needed to complete your pattern.

Custom Design Services: Offer custom pattern design services for customers who have specific project ideas.

Conclusion

Knitting and crochet patterns offer a delightful opportunity to generate income by sharing your passion for crafting. By focusing on a niche, creating well-written and visually appealing patterns, and implementing effective marketing strategies, you can establish a thriving business and inspire countless crafters to bring their creative visions to life.

60. Meditation or Yoga Guides

The growing interest in mindfulness and well-being has fueled the demand for meditation and yoga resources. By offering these practices as digital products, you can share your expertise and generate income by helping others find inner peace and physical balance. Here's a roadmap to cultivating a successful business in this flourishing niche:

The Allure of Digital Guides

Digital meditation and yoga guides offer several advantages for practitioners:

Convenience & Accessibility: Downloadable guides can be accessed anytime, anywhere, on various devices.

Tailored Practices: Cater to specific needs and experience levels with beginner, intermediate, and advanced guides.

Cost-Effective Alternative: Offer a more affordable option compared to in-person classes or workshops.

In-Depth Content: Provide detailed explanations, step-by-step instructions, and modifications for different needs.

Developing Profitable Meditation & Yoga Guides

Identify Your Niche: Focus on specific meditation techniques (mindfulness, guided meditations) or yoga styles (Hatha, Vinyasa).

Clear & Accessible Language: Use clear and concise language that is easy for beginners to understand.

Visually Appealing Design: Incorporate high-quality images, diagrams, and infographics to enhance user experience.

Audio Recordings (Optional): Offer guided meditations with calming narration to deepen the practice.

Monetization Strategies

Direct Sales: Sell individual guides or collections through your website or online marketplaces like Etsy or Amazon Kindle Direct Publishing.

Subscription Model: Offer access to a library of downloadable guides, video tutorials, and audio recordings for a monthly or annual fee.

Freemium Model: Provide a limited sample guide for free and premium versions with more in-depth content and advanced practices.

Additional Considerations

Credibility & Expertise: Highlight your qualifications (yoga teacher certification, meditation experience) to build trust with potential customers.

Marketing & Promotion: Promote your guides through yoga studios, wellness blogs, social media influencers, and online communities.

Community Building: Create a community forum or online course platform to offer ongoing support and interaction with your audience.

Content Variety: Offer different guide formats like written guides, video tutorials, or downloadable audio meditations to cater to diverse learning styles.

Beyond the Basics

Personalized Plans: Develop customized meditation or yoga plans based on individual needs and goals (stress management, improved sleep, etc.).

Live Online Sessions: Complement your digital guides with live online meditation or yoga sessions for a more interactive experience.

Collaboration: Partner with yoga studios or wellness centers to offer online workshops or retreats based on your guides.

Meditation and yoga guides offer a meaningful opportunity to create a successful digital business. By focusing on a specific niche, crafting clear and engaging content, and implementing effective marketing strategies, you can help others cultivate well-being and build a thriving business grounded in mindfulness and holistic health.

Conclusion

As we reach the final pages of "60 Digital Moneymakers: Launch Your Digital Product & Building a Lucrative Empire," I want to express my gratitude for joining this transformative journey. Building a digital empire is not just about making money online; it's about creating a sustainable and fulfilling lifestyle. Remember, each digital product you launch has the power to shape your future, providing not only passive income but a sense of accomplishment.

In the realm of online entrepreneurship, building a brand and connecting with your audience is paramount. Leverage the insights shared within these pages to master the art of marketing automation, pricing strategies, and the legal nuances of selling digital products. Your ability to manage time effectively will become the cornerstone of your success as an online entrepreneur.

Whether you're aspiring to work from home, embrace the digital nomad lifestyle, or simply seek creative business ideas, this book has equipped you with the knowledge to thrive. As you embark on your journey, always remember the importance of continuous learning and adaptation in the ever-evolving digital landscape.

May your digital ventures be prosperous, your brand resonate with authenticity, and your entrepreneurial spirit soar. Here's to building not just a lucrative empire, but a legacy of innovation and success. Thank you for being part of this transformative experience.

With warm regards,
M.I.Fazil